THE HISTORY OF
BRITISH
BIKES

THE HISTORY OF
BRITISH
BIKES

ROLAND BROWN

PARRAGON

This is a Parragon Book

© Parragon 1999

Parragon
Queen Street House
4 Queen Street
Bath BA1 1HE
United Kingdom

Designed, produced and packaged by
Stonecastle Graphics Ltd
Old Chapel Studio, Plain Road, Marden, Tonbridge,
Kent TN12 9LS, United Kingdom

Edited by Philip de Ste. Croix

ISBN 0-75253-153-0

Printed in Italy

Page 1: Norton's desirable 497cc Dominator 88.

Page 2: The ultimate café racer in action; a 650cc Triton.

Page 3: The racy BSA DBD34 Gold Star Clubman's offered enthusiastic amateurs an affordable road and race bike.

Photographic credits:

Andrew Morland: pages 1, 6, 8 (*above*), 8 (*below*), 9, 10 (*below*),
11, 12, 13 (*below*), 14 (*above*), 14 (*below*), 15 (*below*), 16 (*above*),
16 (*below*), 17, 18, 19 (*above*), 19 (*below*), 20 (*below*), 21 (*above*),
21 (*below*), 22, 23 (*above*), 24 (*above*), 24 (*below*), 25 (*below*), 27 (*left*),
27 (*right*), 28 (*above*), 28-29 (*below*), 29 (*right*), 30, 34, 35 (*above*),
35 (*below*), 36 (*right*), 37 (*left*), 37 (*right*), 38, 39 (*above*), 39 (*below*),
40 (*above*), 40 (*below*), 41, 42, 43 (*below*), 45 (*above*), 46-47 (*above*),
49, 52, 54 (*above*), 54 (*below*), 55, 56 (*left*), 56 (*right*), 57 (*left*),
57 (*right*), 60 (*above*), 60 (*below*), 64 (*above*), 64 (*below*), 66 (*above*),
66 (*below*), 70 (*below*), 70-71 (*above*), 73 (*above*), 76, 76-77 (*above*),
77 (*below*), 79 (*left*), 80, 81 (*above*), 81 (*below*), 85 (*above*), 86,
87 (*above*), 87 (*below*), 89 (*above*), 90, 91 (*left*), 91 (*right*), 92 (*right*),
93 (*left*), 93 (*right*), 94, 95 (*above*), 95 (*below*).

Don Morley: pages 13 (*above*), 26 (*left*), 31 (*left*), 31 (*right*),
32 (*above*), 32 (*below*), 36 (*left*), 53 (*left*), 53 (*right*), 58 (*left*), 58 (*right*),
59 (*left*), 59 (*right*), 65 (*above*), 65 (*below*), 68, 69 (*left*), 69 (*right*),
92 (*left*).

Phil Masters/Roland Brown: pages 2, 3, 23 (*below*), 47 (*below*),
50-51 (*below*), 62, 63 (*left*), 63 (*right*), 72, 74, 75 (*left*), 75 (*right*), 78,
79 (*right*), 82 (*left*), 83 (*right*).

Roland Brown: pages 7 (*above*), 10 (*above*), 26 (*right*), 43 (*below*),
48, 51 (*above*), 61, 67, 82-83 (*below*), 84, 85 (*below*), 88, 89 (*below*).

David Goldman/Roland Brown: pages 33 (*above*), 33 (*below*),
50 (*left*).

Paul Bryant/Roland Brown: pages 7 (*below*), 25 (*above*).

P. Gosling/Roland Brown: pages 44, 45 (*below*).

Oli Tennent/Roland Brown: pages 73 (*below*), 83 (*above*).

Jack Burnicle/Roland Brown: page 81 (*left*).

Contents

Introduction

It is satisfying to be able to begin a history of British bikes with the observation that this book is by no means complete. A dozen years or so ago, if would have been possible to write about the British motorcycle industry solely in the past tense, looking back nostalgically at the great machines of years gone by, and lamenting that future production would comprise just a small number of bikes from a handful of specialist firms.

Below: As early as the 1920s, the exotic Brough Superior SS100 V-twin was providing the Nottingham firm's exclusive group of riders with genuine high-performance motorcycling, combining 100mph (161km/h) plus top speed and excellent handling.

*T*RIUMPH'S REMARKABLE rejuvenation in recent years means the story now can have a positive ending. Britain will surely never regain the dominance it enjoyed in the 1950s and '60s, or conceive of manufacturing the huge volume of bikes that were built in those years, but at least we can look forward to many more fine machines from the country that for so long was the world's centre of motorcycle production.

Britain cannot claim to have had much to do with the very earliest motorcycles, which originated mainly in Continental Europe. Michaux-Perreaux of France built the first steam-driven bicycle in 1868. German engineer Gottlieb Daimler created his famous wooden-framed 'Einspur' in 1885. And the world's first production motorcycle, the 1500cc Hildebrand and Wolfmüller of 1894, was also from Germany.

But firms such as Holden, Raleigh and Humber established a British motorcycle industry in the early years of the 20th century, and they were soon followed by a huge number of others. Many produced only a small number of bikes, quickly faded into oblivion

Left: Triumph emphasized its return as a serious manufacturer in 1997, with the launch of the racy T595 Daytona (left) and its unfaired three-cylinder sibling, the T509 Speed Triple.

Below: Another great old British marque, BSA, returned in more modest style in 1999 with the Yamaha-engined Gold SR single.

and have subsequently been forgotten by all but the most dedicated historians. A trip around the National Motorcycle Museum, which is situated near Birmingham, reveals bikes from obscure firms such as Quadrant, Hoskinson, Campion, Hobart and Grigg, to name just a few of a very long list.

A good number of those early manufacturers thrived, however: winning races, setting speed records, and producing huge numbers of machines for sale in Britain and abroad. Many of the early bikes were fairly simple singles and twins, powered by motors from specialists such as JAP and Villiers. But there was plenty of clever engineering, too, notably with Scott's advanced two-strokes.

The 1930s saw British firms take great strides, leading motorcycling's development with a host of notable machines. Triumph's Speed Twin, numerous fine singles from Norton, big V-twins from Brough and Vincent, and Ariel's Square Four provided two-wheeled glamour and performance. And although there was less innovation in the years after the Second World War, the British industry continued to dominate the scene.

There was little sign of decline in the 1950s, when British parallel twins ruled the roads. But the 1960s saw Japanese manufacturers, led by Honda, establish themselves in the market with cleverly engineered machines, initially of small capacity, while the British firms were largely content to tread water, seemingly bereft of imagination or willingness to invest for the future.

By the early 1970s it was almost all over: Honda's CB750 had taken motorcycle design to a new level, while Triumph and BSA — whose own much-delayed Trident/Rocket 3 triple had been overshadowed by the Japanese four — were, like Norton, in serious financial trouble. Other great marques including Ariel, Sunbeam, Brough Superior and Vincent had already disappeared.

Triumph struggled on for the longest, producing increasingly dated parallel twins, before finally going into liquidation in 1983. And there the story might have ended — at least as far as volume production is concerned — were it not for one John Bloor, a self-made building millionaire who bought the Triumph name from the receiver and proceeded to add an unlikely final chapter to the story.

Following the success of Bloor's Triumph during the 1990s, the Hinckley-based firm enters the new millennium with a range of sophisticated superbikes. Add to that BSA's return to production with the single-cylinder Gold SR, the flurry of activity surrounding Norton, plus the work of specialists such as CCM and Harris, and it's clear that the British motorcycle industry has an exciting future to celebrate, as well as a glorious past.

ABC

The many similarities between ABC's 398cc transverse flat-twin of 1920 and BMW's first motorcycle, which appeared with the same engine layout three years later, have led many people to assume that the German firm based its design on the British machine. The truth or otherwise of that assertion will never be known.

*I*T IS certainly true that the machine produced by Granville Bradshaw's All British (Engine) Company was impressively sophisticated. It featured suspension and drum brakes at both front and rear, a tubular-steel cradle frame, four-speed gearbox and multi-plate clutch.

The ABC shared more than its basic engine layout with BMW's R32, too, because both bikes were intended to be built in former aircraft factories – that of Sopwith in Surrey in the case of

the British bike – following the end of the First World War in November 1918. But there were also many differences between the two machines.

While the ABC used overhead valves and a four-speed gearbox with a car-style H-gate shift lever, the BMW was fitted with side valves, and its three-speed transmission was operated by a simple hand change. Perhaps the key difference was that while the German firm took advantage of the longitudinal crankshaft to fit a shaft final

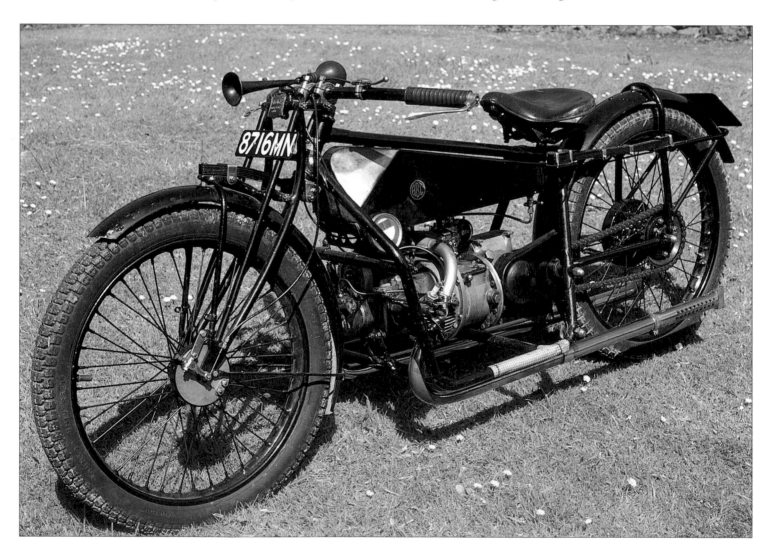

drive system, the British bike turned the drive through 90 degrees and used a chain.

Not that this should imply criticism of the ABC, the rear suspension of which (the R32 had a rigid frame) would have made shaft-drive more complex. In fact Bradshaw was a talented and versatile engineer who had not only designed and built an in-line 494cc flat-twin motorcycle before the War, but had also developed, among many other things, a 400hp aircraft engine with nine radial cylinders, called the Dragonfly.

Much thought went into the design of the transverse flat-twin for which ABC remains best known. The 398cc engine was advanced in having oversquare cylinder dimensions of 68.6 x 54mm. Its cylinders were individually turned from steel billet, and fitted with cast iron heads.

To prevent the ABC's vulnerable transverse cylinders from being damaged when the bike was dropped, Bradshaw protected them by splaying the frame's downtubes outwards. This also facilitated the provision of footboards and weather protection for the rider's legs. Adjustable louvres allowed cooling air to the engine.

SPECIFICATIONS	ABC (1920)
Engine	Air-cooled ohv four-valve flat-twin
Capacity	398cc (68.6 x 54mm)
Maximum power	Not known
Transmission	Four-speed, chain final drive
Frame	Steel twin downtube
Suspension	Leaf-spring front and rear
Brakes	Drum front and rear
Weight	175lb (79kg)
Top speed	60mph (97km/h)

Opposite top: ABC's first V-twin, the 492cc model of 1913, had cylinders in line with the bike. Only small numbers of the 3.5hp twin were built.

Opposite: This sporty 398cc model, dating from 1920, has the transverse V-twin engine for which ABC is known.

Right: The Skootamota was built after the First World War and was powered by a 125cc engine above the rear wheel.

Things looked very promising for ABC when a prototype bike was released to the press for testing early in 1919. *Motor Cycle* magazine reported brisk acceleration, good hill-climbing and a 60mph (97km/h) top speed, plus a smooth and quiet engine. At 175lb (79kg) the twin was light for such a luxurious machine, and its advanced chassis gave good handling and a comfortable ride, with excellent stability at speed.

In addition to being built by Sopwith at Kingston-upon-Thames, the ABC was licensed for production by Gnome et Rhône in France. There was no shortage of orders, but teething problems caused a delay in production. When the bike finally went on sale in May 1920, inflation had increased its price sharply to £160, leading to many cancelled orders.

Most of those who did buy an ABC were impressed, particularly one Jack Emerson, who twice broke the record for distance travelled in an hour, ultimately riding his twin for 70.44 miles (113.36km) in that time at Brooklands. But there were mechanical problems, too, notably with the kickstarter and the valvegear, which was fragile at high revs.

Sadly for ABC, only about 2000 examples of the promising transverse twin were ever built. Ironically BMW, which launched its flat-twin in 1923, is still using the same engine layout successfully more than 75 years later. But by the time the R32 reached the market, the ABC with which it had so much in common was no longer in production.

AJS

Huge numbers of roadgoing bikes were built and sold bearing the AJS name until the mid-1960s, but the marque's most famous machines were racers. The firm from Wolverhampton made its mark in 1914, when its bikes finished first, second, third, fourth and sixth in the Junior TT on the Isle of Man. Later competition machines such as the 7R, Porcupine and 500cc V4 are still remembered – for differing reasons – today.

Above: The Porcupine Model E96.

*A*LBERT JOHN Stevens was a blacksmith's son who founded his company, A.J. Stevens & Co, to build motorcycles in 1909, after supplying small-capacity engines to other firms. Two years later he produced his first machine, a 292cc side-valve roadster, which was entered for the TT. But it was that Isle of Man success three years later, plus three further victories after the First World War, that led to the rapid expansion of AJS.

Success in the 1920s with a variety of side-valve singles led in 1931 to the introduction of the S3, a tourer with a 496cc transverse V-twin engine. Sadly for Stevens, it was expensive to develop and didn't sell. Weakened by an unsuccessful diversification into cars and commercial vehicles, AJS looked set to disappear before being taken over by Matchless, who moved bike production to Plumstead in south London.

The combined firm in turn became part of AMC (Associated Motor Cycles) in 1938, but the AJS and Matchless names were retained and used, in an attempt to attract each brand's enthusiasts. Most of AJS's roadsters were unspectacular singles and parallel twins

such as the Model 20, also called the Matchless G9, which was introduced in 1948 and was inspired – as were so many bikes at that time – by Triumph's successful Speed Twin.

Several AJS racebikes were much more exotic, notably the 500cc V4 of the mid-1930s, which used a supercharger to produce 55hp. Initially air-cooled and unreliable, the V4 improved with liquid cooling and had a top speed of 130mph (209km/h), but was heavy and handled poorly. Although its performance in the Isle of Man was disappointing, the V4 did at least enter the record books when Walter Rusk recorded the first 100mph (161km/h) lap at the Ulster Grand Prix.

Another famous 'Ajay' racer was the Porcupine, a dohc 498cc parallel twin that first appeared in 1947 and was so named because

Opposite: Greatest of all 350cc singles: the 350cc 7R.

Above: Big V-twins included this 1000cc Colonial of 1938.

of the spiky fins on its cylinders. The bike was designed to be boosted by a supercharger, but 'blowers' were banned after the Second World War, and with conventional carburettors the Porcupine was never competitive at the highest level.

The best loved AJS was the 7R, the 350cc single-cylinder racebike that was produced from 1948 to 1962. Nicknamed the 'Boy Racer', the 7R was a relatively simple and inexpensive production racer that was light, agile and fast enough to win countless National-level races.

Its biggest success came in 1952, when Bob McIntyre not only won the Junior Manx Grand Prix, but rode the 350cc 7R to second place against 500cc opposition in the Senior two days later. The 7R was itself enlarged to 500cc to produce the Matchless G50, which was also raced with great success for many years.

AJS also scored a competition victory with one of its best-ever roadsters, the Model 31 CSR of 1960. The sporty parallel twin, also sold as the Matchless G12 CSR, had a top speed of 110mph (177km/h) and won that year's prestigious Thruxton 500-mile race. But that boost was not enough to keep the old marque alive for many more years. Parent company AMC became part of Norton Villiers in 1967, after which the AJS name ceased to be used.

SPECIFICATIONS	AJS 7R (1954)
Engine	Air-cooled ohc two-valve single
Capacity	348cc (74 x 81mm)
Maximum power	37hp @ 7000rpm
Transmission	Four-speed, chain final drive
Frame	Steel twin downtube
Suspension	Telescopic forks; twin rear shocks
Brakes	Drum front and rear
Weight	310lb (141kg)
Top speed	120mph (193km/h)

Ariel Red Hunter

For many years Ariel was one of the most glamorous of British manufacturers. Its advertisements in the early 1950s boasted that the factory at Selly Oak in Birmingham was unique in building four-, twin- and single-cylinder models: 'Whichever Ariel machine is chosen, the rider can be sure of getting the very best of its class – in keeping with that unrivalled reputation for leadership in design and manufacture, which has made Ariel The World's Most Exclusive Motor Cycle.'

Below: In 1937 the 500cc Red Hunter was a simple machine whose chassis combined girder forks and a rigid rear end.

Opposite bottom: The Red Hunter's pushrod single engine was built in capacities of 250cc, 350cc and, as here, 500cc.

*T*HE FIRM'S beginnings were considerably more humble. Ariel built bicycles before producing its first powered vehicle, a De Dion–engined quadricycle, in 1898. A few years later, after being taken over by the Sangster family, Ariel began motorcycle production with a succession of unremarkable side-valve singles and V-twins, some using bought-in engines.

Charles Sangster was a talented engineer and his son Jack, who took over running the firm, had a knack for employing others who were even better. In the 1920s he hired a trio of designers – Valentine Page, Bert Hopwood and Edward Turner – who would all become leading figures in the industry.

In 1926 Page, then Ariel's chief engineer, designed the single-cylinder machine from which the famous Red Hunter was developed six years later. The Red Hunter was a sporting version of Ariel's 500cc ohv single, and the range was later expanded to include 250cc and 350cc models. Grass-track and trials riders

Leader Fails to Save Ariel

One of the boldest machines that Ariel built in its long history was the Leader, an innovative, fully-enclosed 250cc two-stroke that was designed by Val Page and launched in 1958. The Leader was powered by a twin-cylinder engine inspired by the German Adler twin. Distinctive and practical thanks to its pressed-steel frame, efficient weather protection and optional hard panniers, it was unlike any previous bike.

Performance was reasonably lively, with 70mph (113km/h) top speed and agile handling. But starting could be troublesome, and the Leader's mediocre brakes and finish did nothing to help it sell in any great numbers. A more conventional looking sports model, the Arrow, was more popular, and the motor was also tuned to give 20hp for a super-sports Golden Arrow version. But Ariel's two-stroke gamble failed, and production ended in 1965.

appreciated the single immediately, and continued to do so for years. Trials legend Sammy Miller's famous Ariel with its 'GOV132' plate was based on a 500cc Red Hunter from 1955.

After Edward Turner had revamped the Hunter with more chrome and brighter paintwork, it rapidly became a hit with road riders too. With a top speed of over 70mph (113km/h) and good handling from its girder-fork chassis, a 350cc Red Hunter was a fine bike by mid-1930s standards. Ten years later it had been improved by the introduction of rear suspension and telescopic forks; by the early 1950s it had an aluminium cylinder head and new frame too.

Page returned to Ariel after the Second World War, and designed a new generation of parallel twins. The reliable but rather dull 500cc KH was not a success. But the 650cc Huntmaster, which combined a modified BSA A10 engine (Ariel had been part of the BSA Group since 1944) with a new frame, became popular, especially with sidecar riders, following its release in 1954.

SPECIFICATIONS	NH350 RED HUNTER (1937)
Engine	Air-cooled ohv two-valve single
Capacity	347cc (72 x 85mm)
Maximum power	17bhp @ 5600rpm
Transmission	Four-speed, chain final drive
Frame	Steel single downtube
Suspension	Girder front forks; solid rear
Brakes	Drum front and rear
Weight	352lb (160kg)
Top speed	80mph (129km/h)

Ariel Square Four

The story of the Ariel's most famous model begins with a young London engineer named Edward Turner sketching his idea for a novel 'square four' engine design on the back of a pack of Wild Woodbine cigarettes, then offering it to a succession of motorcycle firms without success. But Ariel boss Jack Sangster liked the idea and gave a job to Turner, whose career at the Selly Oak firm and at Triumph (where he created the Speed Twin, among others) would mark him as arguably the greatest of all British designers.

Above: The Mk I Square Four featured exhaust manifolds in the head, and twin downpipes.

*T*HE SQUARE four layout consisted essentially of a pair of parallel twins, sharing a common crankcase, cylinder block and head, and with their crankshafts geared together. This gave the advantages of four-cylinder power and smoothness in a unit that was so compact that it could be fitted into a frame very similar to that used for Ariel's 500cc single.

Drawbacks were high production costs and the difficulty of providing adequate cooling for the sheltered rear cylinders – a problem that was to dog the 'Squariel'

for all of its remarkably long life. The Square Four was built between 1931 and 1958. It changed greatly during that time but remained throughout a unique and desirable machine.

Turner's original model, launched to great acclaim at the Olympia Motorcycle Show in 1930, had a capacity of 497cc, and a chain-driven overhead camshaft. Its exhaust manifolds were integral with the cylinder head, so only two exhaust pipes emerged from the engine, leading to a pair of fishtail silencers. The chassis comprised a hard-tail frame with girder forks, and drum brakes.

Above: By 1952 the Square Four had a 997cc engine, telescopic front forks and plunger rear suspension.

In 1932 the motor was bored out to 597cc, giving more power for use with a sidecar. In this form the Square Four produced 24hp at 6000rpm, and remained impressively smooth to its top speed of 85mph (137km/h). But the engine design gave numerous problems which, after Turner's departure, were addressed by new chief engineer Val Page with revised 597cc and 997cc versions that were introduced in 1937.

The new engines featured more cylinder head finning, plus a tunnel between the cylinders to allow cooling air to circulate to the rear of the block. Other changes included pushrod valve operation, longer stroke dimensions, redesigned crankshafts and a new Solex carburettor placed conventionally behind the motor, in place of the original bike's forward-mounted Amal.

In its new large-capacity guise the Square Four produced 38hp with plenty of low-down torque, making it ideal for use with a sidecar. Ariel's advertising line: 'Ten to a hundred in top gear' rang

SPECIFICATIONS	ARIEL SQUARE FOUR (1932)
Engine	Air-cooled ohv eight-valve square four
Capacity	597cc (56 x 61mm)
Maximum power	24hp @ 6000rpm
Transmission	Four-speed, chain final drive
Frame	Steel twin downtube
Suspension	Girder forks; rigid rear
Brakes	Drum front and rear
Weight	413lb (187kg)
Top speed	85mph (137km/h)

true – top speed was just over 100mph (161km/h). But as well as some lingering mechanical unreliability the larger Four also suffered from mediocre handling, being too heavy for the plunger rear suspension system that by then had been adopted along with telescopic forks at the front.

Square Four Mk II: the Ultimate Tourer

Ariel reduced weight and improved cooling after the Second World War with a new all-aluminium engine, and in 1953 introduced the comprehensively revised 4G Mk II model. This was a handsome machine with a larger, rounded petrol tank and a further updated engine featuring four separate exhaust downpipes.

Even in this final form the engine was prone to overheat in traffic, and the Mk II's handling was not a match for the smooth and powerful engine. Ariel deemed further redevelopment too costly, and abandoned production in 1958. But the Square Four's reputation lived on. Fast, smooth and luxurious, it was the ultimate tourer of its day.

Below: The Square Four Mk II was easily distinguishable from its predecessor by the pair of exhaust downpipes that emerged from each side of the engine. Like the Mk I model, it was ideally suited to pulling a sidecar.

Ascot-Pullin 500

The 500cc single produced by racer and engineer Cyril Pullin in 1928 deserved to be a success, for its long list of advanced features alone. With a pressed-steel frame, fully enclosed drive chain, comprehensive instrument panel, quickly detachable wheels, hydraulically operated linked drum brakes, plus options including legshields, windscreen and even a wiper, the Ascot-Pullin was in many respects ahead of its time.

HERTFORDSHIRE-BASED Pullin had previously attempted to produce an unconventional roadster with his Pullin-Groome of a few years earlier. This had a less substantial pressed-steel frame that enclosed a 216cc single-cylinder engine, positioned horizontally. But the bike's sophistication held little appeal for many motorcyclists, and it proved too expensive and untried to sell in great numbers.

The Ascot-Pullin's engine was a 496cc overhead-valve unit, its cylinder again lying horizontally and its unit-construction gearbox situated above the crankcase. Petrol and oil tanks were located above, inside the framework. The twin-port cylinder head fed a pair of large exhaust pipes, one on each side of the bike. The three-speed gearbox was operated by a hand lever, also on the right.

With an output of about 17hp, the Ascot-Pullin had a top speed of 70mph (113km/h). At 330lb (150kg) the single was fairly light too, despite the rather heavy appearance given by its full bodywork. However, the Ascot-Pullin was no more of a success than its predecessor, and production ended only a couple of years later.

Above and below: Futuristic features did not make the Ascot-Pullin a hit.

SPECIFICATIONS	ASCOT-PULLIN (1928)
Engine	Air-cooled ohv two-valve single
Capacity	496cc (82 x 94mm)
Maximum power	17hp (estimated)
Transmission	Three-speed, chain final drive
Frame	Pressed steel
Suspension	Pressed-steel girder front; rigid rear
Brakes	Drum front and rear
Weight	330lb (150kg)
Top speed	70mph (113km/h) approx

Bond

The name Bond is best known for the distinctive three-wheeled 'Bond Bug' cars that were popular in some circles in the 1970s, but Lawrence Bond also created a motorcycle that was every bit as unusual. His single-cylinder bike was based around a large, tapered tube of oval-section aluminium sheet, which was rolled into shape and riveted along the seam on its underside.

Below: With its enclosed wheels, balloon tyres, legshields and tubular, sheet-aluminium frame, the Villiers-engined Bond was one of the strangest bikes on the road in 1951.

*T*HIS TUBULAR frame was cut away at the 'sharp' rear end to make room for the back wheel, and stiffened by a huge rear mudguard that hid most of the wheel from view. The front wheel was obscured by an even larger mudguard of similar construction. Despite the appearance of telescopic forks, the tubes were initially unsprung, as was the rear end, so the Bond relied for comfort on its sprung saddle and 16-inch balloon tyres.

Large legshields, painted in matching light blue, reached down from the frame to the bike's footboards. The engine, which hung from the main frame beam, was initially the 99cc Villiers 1F two-stroke with a two-speed gearbox. In 1951 this model was joined by a de luxe version powered by a 125cc JAP engine with a three-speed gearbox. By this time telescopic forks were fitted.

The strange single was initially built in Lancashire by the Bond Aircraft and Engineering Company. But in 1951 a Yorkshire firm, Ellis, took over while Bond produced a variety of lightweight bikes and scooters

SPECIFICATIONS	BOND (1950)
Engine	Air-cooled two-stroke single
Capacity	99cc
Maximum power	Not known
Transmission	Two-speed, chain final drive
Frame	Aluminium monocoque
Suspension	Rigid front and rear
Brakes	Drum front and rear
Weight	90lb (41kg)
Top speed	45mph (72km/h) approx

under the name BAC. Ellis made a few minor frame alterations, but the bikes were not a great success and production ended in 1954. The company later relocated to Preston in Lancashire and built scooters for a few years, before abandoning them to concentrate on three-wheeler production in 1962.

Brough Superior

One marque stood out above all others in the 1920s and '30s: Brough Superior. The machines built by George Brough and his small team in their workshop at Haydn Road, Nottingham were mostly exotic, costly and rapid V-twins – superbikes, decades before the term had even been invented.

Below: This 1932-model SS100 was owned by Lawrence of Arabia.

Opposite below: Like the SS100, the SS80 was powered by a big V-twin engine.

GEORGE BROUGH was an outstanding rider as well as engineer, and won many races, sprints and hillclimbs – as did other notable Brough riders including Eric Fernihough, Freddie Dixon and Bert Le Vack. Brough was also a great publicist, naming his marque Brough Superior to the annoyance of his father, who produced flat-twins and whose comment was: 'I suppose that makes mine the Brough Inferior?'

George Brough's aim was to build 'a big solo machine, made up to an ideal and not down to a price'. With ownership came membership of an unofficial club of which he was the captain. His most famous customer was the British soldier and author T.E. Lawrence, Lawrence of Arabia, who owned a special stainless steel petrol tank that he fitted to his series of Broughs, and who was killed in 1935 when he crashed while riding one.

The company's slogan was 'The Rolls-Royce of Motorcycles', borrowed from a comment made in an early Brough test published by *The Motor Cycle* magazine. The car firm's initial objection to the use of its name was withdrawn after a Rolls executive had arrived at Haydn Road to find workers wearing white gloves to avoid marking the show bikes they were assembling!

Brough's Fantastic Fours

George Brough was supremely aware of the value of publicity, and used the annual British motorcycle show to reveal a string of innovative four-cylinder machines. Two fours that were displayed to great acclaim in successive late-1920s shows failed to reach production. In 1931 Brough revealed another four, powered by a modified 796cc engine from the Austin Seven car. With shaft drive to twin rear wheels, it was intended for use with a sidecar. Only ten were built, partly because the authorities declared that when fitted with a sidecar the Brough had four wheels, so it should be taxed at the higher car rate.

In 1938 an even more stunning machine was unveiled on the Nottingham firm's show stand. The Brough Superior Dream, also known as the Golden Dream, was a 998cc flat-four with cylinders arranged like two flat-twins placed one above the other. Twin crankshafts were linked by gears and rotated in opposite directions making the bike supremely smooth. Development was halted by the outbreak of the Second World War, and Brough did not resume production afterwards.

Above: Brough's Austin Seven-engined four of the early 1930s was purpose-built for sidecar use, with twin rear wheels.

An estimated 3000 Brough Superiors were built during the firm's two decades in business. Best known are the SS80, named after its 80mph (129km/h) top speed, and the even more famous SS100, which was produced between 1925 and 1940. Powered initially by a 980cc V-twin from J.A. Prestwich (JAP) of north London, the SS100 came with a signed guarantee from Brough that the bike had been timed at over 100mph (161km/h) for a quarter of a mile. Brochures boasted of 'hands-off stability at 95mph' (153km/h).

Fewer than 400 examples of the SS100 were built. As with all Broughs, their specifications varied considerably. Most were powered by JAP engines but the last 100 or so models used an AMC (Matchless) V-twin. Notable variants included the SS100 Alpine Grand Sports, built for fast touring, and the racing Pendine, with high-compression engine, rear-set footrests and guarantee of 110mph (177km/h) performance.

SPECIFICATIONS	BROUGH SUPERIOR SS100 (1925)
Engine	Air-cooled four-valve ohv pushrod 50-degree V-twin
Capacity	988cc (85.5 x 86mm)
Maximum power	45bhp @ 5000rpm
Transmission	Four-speed, chain final drive
Frame	Steel single downtube
Suspension	Girder forks; rigid rear
Brakes	Drum front and rear
Weight	396lb (180kg)
Top speed	100mph (161km/h)

BSA Model E

BSA was for many years the largest of all Britain's motorcycle manufacturers. It was also one of the oldest, with origins dating back to the 1850s, when gunsmiths from the Birmingham area formed a trade association. In 1861 they founded the Birmingham Small Arms Company to produce guns in a factory at Small Heath in the south of the city.

*T*HE FIRM turned to bicycle production in the 1880s, to keep busy in peacetime. Then, in the early 1900s, BSA began building motorcycles, using engines from firms including Minerva of Belgium. In 1910 the firm built its first complete motorbike: a 499cc side-valve single that produced 3.5hp and sold for £50. Helped by its respectable performance and BSA's well-known name, it was a success.

BSA's reputation grew in the 1920s with a series of popular V-twins, beginning with the Model E. This had a 770cc engine, with

Right: BSA continued its production of big V-twins into the 1930s with machines such as this 986cc model from 1932.

Below: The 770cc Model E, introduced in 1919, was a success due largely to its reliability and cheap price.

The Round Tank was one of the stars of a notable 1924 publicity stunt in which a group of BSA riders made a mass ascent of Snowdon mountain in north Wales. The success of this event contrasted with the expensive disaster of three years earlier, when a team of six riders had entered the Isle of Man TT on innovative single-cylinder racers. All of the fast but under-developed bikes broke down, after which BSA abandoned racing for many years.

One of the Snowdon event riders was star designer Harold Briggs, whose Sloper single – so called on account of its angled-forward single cylinder – was another of BSA's most popular early models. The first Sloper, the S27, was launched in 1926 powered by a very quiet 493cc overhead-valve engine. The bike featured a twin-downtube frame and BSA's first modern-style 'saddle' type fuel tank.

BSA also built 350cc and 600cc versions of the Sloper, production of which continued well into the 1930s. For sportier riders the firm also offered the Blue Star range, complete with upright, slightly tuned, vertical single-cylinder engines. These were developed from the machine ridden by BSA's trials ace (and later Competitions Manager) Bert Perrigo, who received a halfpenny royalty on each Blue Star sold.

The Second World War was a busy time for the BSA factory which, despite suffering heavy bomb damage that claimed 53 workers' lives, produced huge numbers of guns and bikes. The two-wheeled mainstay was the 500cc single-cylinder M20, designed by former Triumph man Val Page. The side-valve M20 was a modest performer, but it was robust and easy to manufacture. The 126,000 M20s built during the war years accounted for a quarter of Britain's motorcycle production, leading to the proud advertising line: 'One in Four was a BSA'.

cylinders angled at 50 degrees. Its 6hp output was enough for a top speed of about 55mph (89km/h). The Model E had a three-speed gearbox, with primary and final drive chains enclosed in an aluminium case. The bike was aimed very much at family sidecar riders; BSA also offered a matching chair in the firm's green and cream colours.

By the mid-1920s BSA had begun using mass-production methods, notably with the Model B or 'Round Tank' model. This was a simple and inexpensive 250cc side-valve single with a two-speed gearbox, and was particularly favoured by learners and delivery riders. The first Round Tanks had hand and foot brakes that both slowed the rear wheel. Later models featured a brake on each wheel, and a three-speed gearbox.

SPECIFICATIONS	BSA MODEL E (1920)
Engine	Air-cooled side-valve V-twin
Capacity	770cc (76 x 85mm)
Maximum power	6hp
Transmission	Three-speed, chain final drive
Frame	Steel diamond
Suspension	Girder front; rigid rear
Brakes	Shoe front and rear
Weight	350lb (159kg)
Top speed	55mph (89km/h)

Above: This M20 military single is painted in desert colours.

BSA Gold Star

During the 1950s BSA was the biggest motorcycle manufacturer in the world, producing over 75,000 bikes in some years. The company was an industrial giant, involved in making guns, taxi-cabs and metal plate as well as motorbikes, and it had taken over the Triumph, Ariel and Sunbeam marques.

Below: Classical lines of the 500cc DBD34 Clubman's Goldie, the ultimate 1950s single.
Opposite top: The humble Bantam was sometimes used for trials competition.
Opposite below: Low clip-on handlebars give the DBD34 a purposeful look.

*B*SA's MOST famous model during that period was the Gold Star. The 'Goldie' had its origins in 1937, when racer Walter Handley earned a Brooklands Gold Star award for lapping the banked track at over 100mph (161km/h) on BSA's 500cc Empire Star. In the following year BSA produced a replica that was marketed under the name M24 Gold Star.

The new name not only recalled Handley's award, but signified that each machine had been individually built out of selected components, tuned and bench-tested, with polished valve ports, con-rods, flywheels and crankcases. Power output was 28hp when fuelled by petrol, or 33hp when tuned to run on alcohol. Buyers received a certified power chart for their machines, a custom that was maintained with Gold Stars throughout.

That first Gold Star also featured magnesium gearbox casings and an aluminium cylinder head and barrel, which had not been seen before in a mass-produced bike. But BSA management decided that to reduce costs the sports Gold Star should resemble the standard single as much as possible, so its chassis was little changed.

After the Second World War, BSA produced a competition bike called the B32, based on its rather ordinary pushrod single, the B31.

Cheap and Cheerful: BSA's Bantam

In contrast to the glamorous Gold Star, BSA's other best-loved model of the 1950s and early 1960s was the Bantam: a humble 125cc two-stroke single whose greatest assets were simplicity, reliability and economy. The Bantam was essentially a copy of German firm DKW's RT125 model, and was acquired as part of the settlement of war reparations.

When launched by BSA in 1946 the Bantam was painted all in green, and had a three-speed gearbox and no rear suspension. Its 4.5hp engine gave a top speed of just over 50mph (80km/h). Over the years the Bantam was uprated with rear shocks and a four-speed box, before finally being dropped in 1971. Most were ridden on the road, but the single was also used for trials and even road-racing.

This was initially made for use in trials, but when fitted with an aluminium cylinder head and barrel its racing potential was clear. In 1949 this bike led to the sporty 350cc ZB32 Gold Star, which was followed a year later by a 500cc version, the ZB34.

Suddenly the enthusiastic amateur (or 'clubman') racer had a cheap bike that could be used for road-riding and racing, and which with a little work was competitive against more exotic machinery. In the early 1950s the Gold Star totally dominated both the 350cc Junior and 500cc Senior Clubman's TT races. BSA's chief designer Bert Hopwood uprated its engine throughout the decade, notably in 1954 with the CB32 and CB34 Gold Star models, which featured new top-ends with large finned cylinders.

Most people's idea of a Gold Star is the DBD34 Clubman's, the racy, top-of-the-range version of the 500cc model released in 1956. With clip-on handlebars, big 1.5in (38mm) Amal Grand Prix carburettor, swept-back exhaust pipe, 42hp maximum power output and a true top speed of 110mph (177km/h), the DBD34 Clubman's was hard to beat on road or track. Gold Star production ended in 1963 but the single remains highly prized today, with good examples costing as much as modern superbikes.

SPECIFICATIONS	BSA DBD34 GOLD STAR CLUBMAN'S (1956)
Engine	Air-cooled ohv two-valve pushrod single
Capacity	499cc (85 x 88mm)
Maximum power	42hp @ 7000rpm
Transmission	Four-speed, chain final drive
Frame	Steel twin downtube
Suspension	Telescopic front; twin shocks rear
Brakes	Drum front and rear
Weight	384lb (174kg)
Top speed	110mph (177km/h)

BSA A10 Golden Flash

BSA joined the trend towards parallel-twin engines rather belatedly in 1946, with the 500cc A7. The new BSA differed from Triumph's hugely successful Speed Twin, which had begun the revolution nine years earlier, by using one camshaft instead of two. Although the A7 was not the fastest or most handsome twin on the market, it was at least quiet, oil-tight and relatively reliable.

Above: BSA's 500cc A7 was similar in most respects to the 650cc A10.

*I*T DIDN'T take BSA long to realize that a larger-engined model was required, especially for use with a sidecar. Designer Bert Hopwood had joined the company in early 1949 and was given the job of enlarging the A7. Hopwood worked frantically to complete his 646cc A10 design in just four weeks. Prototypes were tested in record time, and the Golden Flash was in production by November the same year.

Despite its hurried development, the Flash was a hit. Its 35hp engine was reasonably smooth, torquey and reliable. The chassis originally incorporated plunger rear suspension, with the option of a rigid frame for sidecar use. The more modern system of swing-arm and twin shock absorbers was introduced in 1954, when other changes included a new gearbox that was still separate from the engine unit.

Above: Despite its rapid development the A10 Golden Flash was a great success, with its 35hp engine producing a top speed of 96mph (154km/h).

BSA Returns with a New Single

The BSA name resurfaced in the late 1970s, when management organized a buyout from Norton Villiers Triumph. The new BSA firm built mopeds and children's bikes, plus Yamaha-engined utility machines that were sold to aid workers in Third World countries. In 1994 the company was bought by the Regal Group, a Southampton-based concern with interests in a variety of areas including engineering, building and electronics.

In 1998 BSA Regal developed a retro-styled roadster, the Gold SR, which combined Gold Star styling, an air-cooled 400cc single-cylinder Yamaha engine (from the Japan-only SR400 model) and a BSA-built frame. The 200 bikes produced that year were all sold to retro-crazy Japan. But in 1999 the Gold SR was given a larger 500cc engine, and put on general sale. BSA was back, albeit on a very modest scale.

In 1962 the A7 and A10 models were replaced by the 500cc A50 and 650cc A65, featuring a unit-construction engine and gearbox. Both models were shorter and lighter than their predecessors, and had improved electrics. But performance and handling were unexceptional, and public reaction was lukewarm.

Interest in BSA's twins increased in 1964 with the introduction of the first sports model, the A65 Rocket, whose 105mph (169km/h) top speed and aggressive looks proved popular. The twin-carburettor A65 Lightning of the following year was faster still and, like its 500cc stablemate the A50 Cyclone, was also available in Clubman's trim with clip-ons, rear-sets, close-ratio box and bench-tested engine.

Most powerful and racy of all the mid-1960s BSAs was the A65 Spitfire Mk II, introduced in 1966 with a bright red petrol tank, high-compression 54hp engine and genuine 120mph (193km/h) top speed. Unfortunately it ran poorly at low revs, vibrated excessively at high revs and was very fragile. Later versions had slightly detuned engines and uprated chassis.

The American market became increasingly important for BSA in the mid-1960s, and sales remained strong. But by the end of the decade the firm was in financial trouble. The situation rapidly worsened as BSA was unable to produce modern bikes to replace its ageing singles and twins, and wasted money with doomed projects such as the 350 Fury twin and Ariel 3 scooter.

BSA's 750cc Rocket 3 triple, developed alongside Triumph's Trident and launched in 1969, was fast and handled well. But its failure to match the sophistication of Honda's rival CB750 highlighted the relative fortunes of the British and Japanese industries. BSA was swallowed up by the new Norton Villiers Triumph Company, and production at Small Heath ended in 1973.

Above: BSA's 1999-model Gold SR resembles the legendary Gold Star.

Below: The 1970's Rocket 3 triple was similar to Triumph's Trident.

SPECIFICATIONS	BSA A10 GOLDEN FLASH (1950)
Engine	Air-cooled ohv four-valve parallel twin
Capacity	646cc (70 x 84mm)
Maximum power	35hp @ 5500rpm
Transmission	Four-speed, chain final drive
Frame	Steel cradle
Suspension	Telescopic front; plunger or rigid rear
Brakes	Drum front and rear
Weight	408lb (185kg)
Top speed	96mph (154km/h)

CCM

The story of CCM, or Clews Competition Machines, began in a lock-up garage in Bolton, Lancashire in 1971 after international motocross racer Alan Clews had bought the contents of ailing BSA's competition department. Clews designed and built a BSA-based 490cc off-roader, intending to ride it himself. But before he could do so, someone offered to buy it. The same thing happened when he built another – and before long CCM was a successful company producing up to a total of 200 off-road bikes per year.

Below left: Trials ace Dave Thorpe puts a 350cc CCM through its paces in 1969. Off-road bikes remain the Lancashire firm's speciality.

Below right: Revitalized CCM launched its first roadgoing model, the 604R, at the Birmingham Show in 1998.

*I*N 1980 Clews sold 90 per cent of CCM to car components firm Armstrong, which increased production to 1000 machines per year. CCM Armstrong built military bikes powered by 493cc four-stroke single engines from Rotax of Austria. The company also produced several different models, powered by 125cc two-stoke and 250cc and 500cc four-stroke engines, that sold in Canada and America under the name Can-Am.

Competition remained important to CCM Armstrong, whose bikes were used successfully in road-racing and trials as well as motocross. Steve Tonkin won the Junior TT on a Rotax-engined 250cc twin in 1981, Niall Mackenzie and Donny McLeod won 250cc and 350cc national titles on similar machines, and Steve Saunders added two British trials championships. The British firm

also built a 350cc road-racer that combined its own 80hp 350cc, in-line twin, two-stroke engine with an advanced carbon-fibre chassis.

Founder Clews bought back the company from Armstrong in 1987, continuing to produce off-road bikes on a smaller scale. In 1998 CCM Motorcycles, boosted by new management and an injection of capital, unveiled its first ever road bike, the 604R, powered by a 597cc single-cylinder Rotax engine.

SPECIFICATIONS	CCM 604R (1999)
Engine	Air-cooled sohc four-valve single
Capacity	597cc (97 x 81mm)
Maximum power	50bhp @ 7000rpm
Transmission	Six-speed, chain final drive
Frame	Steel twin cradle
Suspension	Telescopic forks front; monoshock rear
Brakes	Single disc front and rear
Weight	370lb (168kg)
Top speed	100mph (161km/h)

Douglas

Douglas is best remembered for roadgoing motorbikes powered by flat-twin engines, but there was a great deal more to the Bristol firm than that. As well as producing speedway motorcycles and TT-winning road-racers, Douglas also built cars, trucks, aeroplane engines and farm tractors.

Below left: A Douglas rider enjoying his 348cc flat-twin on the Banbury Run.
Below right: The smooth and stylish Dragonfly failed to save Douglas.

THE FLAT-twin was the Douglas trademark, from the first bike completed in 1907 to the final model more than half a century later. The Douglas company had begun in foundry work before becoming involved with engineering. That first model's engine, a 350cc twin with cylinders in-line, was designed by Joseph Barter from his own previous design, which he had marketed under the name Fairy.

Early Douglas highlights included winning the team prize in the International Six Days Trial in 1910, and a first TT victory in the Junior event two years later. In 1923 Douglas won not only the Senior TT, but also the sidecar event with a banked outfit piloted by Freddie Dixon. But the company also suffered a series of well-publicized financial crises and relaunches.

After the Second World War, Douglas produced a new line of flat-twins with transverse cylinders, commencing with the 350cc T35 of 1947. The 1950 range included two sports machines: the 90 Plus, built almost to racing standards, and the lower specification 80

SPECIFICATIONS	DOUGLAS DRAGONFLY (1955)
Engine	Air-cooled ohv four-valve flat-twin
Capacity	348cc (60.8 x 60mm)
Maximum power	17hp @ 6000rpm
Transmission	Four-speed, chain final drive
Frame	Steel twin downtube
Suspension	Earles-type forks; twin shock rear
Brakes	Drum front and rear
Weight	365lb (166kg)
Top speed	75mph (121km/h)

Plus. Although performance was generally good, the twins gained a reputation for dubious quality of workmanship and materials.

The last and best of the twins was the 350cc Dragonfly, which was launched in 1955 and featured a distinctive headlamp nacelle that blended into the fuel tank. The Dragonfly cruised smoothly at 60mph (97km/h), and handled well thanks to its Earles fork chassis. But the twin was heavy, expensive and not particularly fast. A promising 500cc prototype never reached the market, and Douglas ceased production in 1957.

Excelsior

Britain's motorcycle industry began in 1896, when Bayliss, Thomas & Co, makers of Excelsior bicycles, began building and selling a machine powered by a 1.25hp Minerva engine from Belgium. In that same year the firm also built its first motor bicycle with the name Excelsior, introducing the machine at the Crystal Palace exhibition in south London and offering free rides to anyone who dared try it.

*B*Y 1902 the Coventry firm was producing machines with 2.75hp engines from MMC, essentially a locally built version of the popular De Dion unit from France. The engine was hung at an angle from the front downtube of a strengthened bicycle-style frame. Drive to the rear wheel was by belt, and the machine had pedals fitted both to help starting and to assist the engine on hills.

In 1910 the company's name was changed to Excelsior, following the demise of a German manufacturer of that name. To avoid confusion both with that company and the American Excelsior firm, the British bikes were also known as 'Bayliss, Thomas' in some countries. Some early machines were produced with unusually large 650cc (4.5hp) and 850cc (5.6hp) single-cylinder engines, while rival firm's units of that size were generally V-twins. Excelsior also built a big V-twin in 1916.

Shortly after the Second World War the company was bought by the Walker family, who moved production to Birmingham and built up a range of bikes from 98cc to 1000cc in capacity. The new directors believed in the value of racing, and Excelsior gained its first major success when Leslie Crabtree won the Lightweight TT at record speed in 1929. The Walkers were quick to exploit this success with a TT Replica, the B14, which cost £78 compared with the £40 of the standard 250cc model.

Excelsior came close to setting a world speed record in 1931, when its Silver Comet, powered by a supercharged 1000cc JAP V-twin engine, clocked 163mph (262km/h) but was unable to complete the necessary return run to ratify the attempt. Most of the firm's bikes were of smaller capacity, notably the exotic 250cc racer known as the 'Mechanical Marvel' due to its complex twin-carb, twin-cam radial four-valve cylinder head, on which Syd Gleave won the Lightweight TT in 1933.

The Mechanical Marvel was thought too complex to be reproduced for public consumption, and instead Excelsior produced a much simpler 250cc machine. The Manxman, designed by Ike Hatch, had two valves and a single overhead camshaft driven from a vertical shaft. Although it never won a TT race, the Manxman's performance and reliability made it very popular with club racers. It was also produced in 350cc and 500cc capacities, though without achieving the same level of racing success.

During the Second World War Excelsior produced the Welbike, a compact folding affair, powered by a 98cc two-stroke engine, that was dropped in a container along with paratroopers to increase their mobility. The bike's success allowed Excelsior to expand and make some of its own engines. It was also produced in revised civilian form after the war, marketed as the Corgi or 'pocket prodigy' by Brockhouse Engineering.

Excelsior's best known post-war model was the Talisman, a two-stroke parallel twin that was launched in 1950, initially in 250cc capacity. The bike produced 12hp and had modest performance, with a top speed of 60mph (97km/h), but it was light and handled well. Despite that, neither the standard Talisman nor the twin-carb STT1 Sports model, introduced in 1952, was a great success. A 350cc version introduced with the S8 model in 1958 failed to turn the tide, as did a 150cc scooter called the Monarch. Production ended when the Walker family sold out to the car accessory firm Britax.

SPECIFICATIONS	EXCELSIOR MANXMAN 250 (1936)
Engine	Air-cooled ohv two-valve single
Capacity	246cc (63 x 79mm)
Maximum power	22hp approx
Transmission	Four-speed, chain final drive
Frame	Steel single cradle
Suspension	Girder front; rigid rear
Brakes	Drum front and rear
Weight	290lb (132kg)
Top speed	80mph (129km/h)

All pictures: The Manxman did not repeat the TT victory of Excelsior's radial four-valve Mechanical Marvel, but the simpler sohc single was a popular and successful racer in the 1930s, especially in the 250cc form shown here. Its vertical single cylinder was notable for the three-legged Manx symbol cast into its bevel gear housing. As with most machines of its day, the chassis combined girder front suspension with a rigid rear end. This machine also has a sprung saddle for added rider comfort.

EMC

Austrian-born two-stroke tuning wizard Dr Joe Ehrlich came to England in the 1930s and founded the Ehrlich Motor Company in west London after the Second World War. Ehrlich was an advocate of the unusual split-single two-stroke engine, and his 350cc EMC machines were powered by such a device. The cylinder block contained two separate in-line bores with a shared combustion chamber. Pistons rose and fell together, linked by a wishbone-shaped conrod.

Below: EMC's sluggish 350cc split-single roadsters of the late 1940s and early 1950s had little of the glamour that became associated with several of Ehrlich's racing ventures, notably Mike Hailwood's fifth in the 125cc world championship in 1962.

*E*HRLICH CLAIMED that the split-single arrangement was superior to conventional engines in its control of the exhaust and transfer ports, but his powerplant was heavy and slow-revving, and rarely lived up to EMC's claims of outstanding fuel economy. The touring Model T, which produced 16hp, and sports Model S, which was 2hp more powerful, were also relatively expensive when introduced in 1947. Nevertheless EMC produced about 1500 before production ended six years later.

Dr Joe later took an engineering job at De Havilland aircraft company, and convinced the firm to fund a 125cc racing effort under the EMC name. Mike Hailwood finished fifth in the 125cc world championship on the bike in 1962. Ehrlich then set up a two-stroke research establishment, equipped with dynamometers and rolling roads, that attracted customers from the worlds of car and power-boat racing.

Ehrlich returned to bikes in the early 1980s, when he joined with the south London-based Waddon Group to launch the Waddon-Ehrlich racing venture. The firm's 250cc machines, powered by modified Rotax engines, were competitive in some high-level international events including Daytona. But grand prix success proved more elusive and a projected road bike did not reach

production. The irrepressible Ehrlich, now well into his eighties, was still making headlines in 1995 but yet another planned EMC comeback failed to materialize.

SPECIFICATIONS	EMC 350 MODEL T (1947)
Engine	Air-cooled two-stroke split-single
Capacity	348cc (50/50 x 88mm)
Maximum power	16hp @ 4500rpm
Transmission	Four-speed, chain final drive
Frame	Steel cradle
Suspension	Telescopic front; plunger rear
Brakes	Drum front and rear
Weight	342lb (155kg)
Top speed	70mph (113km/h)

Francis-Barnett

'Fanny-B' (as the company was fondly nicknamed) was founded after Gordon Francis, son of Graham Francis of Lea-Francis motorcycle manufacturing fame, had married the daughter of Arthur Barnett, builder of Invicta bikes. The new groom and his father-in-law teamed up and began production in the Coventry factory made available by Excelsior's recent move to Birmingham.

Below left: The 1934 Lapwing combined a 147cc engine with a frame of bolted-together steel tubes.
Below right: The original Cruiser of the 1930s was a 250cc single with pressed-steel legshields.

FRANCIS-BARNETT is remembered as one of motorcycling's less glamorous marques but that was not the whole story. Its first model, announced in 1920, was powered by a 292cc side-valve JAP engine. The bike shared its frame with Barnett's Invicta model but was slightly classier, with toe-shields incorporated into its footboards, a cast-alloy instead of pressed-steel chain cover – and its price listed in guineas instead of pounds.

Before long, though, Francis and Barnett were producing a low-cost utility bike combining Gordon Francis's innovative frame, made from bolted-together steel tubes, with a 150cc Villiers two-stroke engine. Advertising boasted that the bike was 'built like a bridge'. The more upmarket Model 10 or Pullman featured a similar chassis with a 344cc twin-cylinder engine.

The striking Cruiser model, introduced in 1933, combined its 250cc Villiers single engine with pressed-steel leg-shields, large mudguards and partial engine covers. Performance was modest but the bike allowed comfortable all-weather touring. The Cruiser name was the firm's best known, also being used on a string of two-stroke singles and twins after the Second World War.

In 1947 Francis-Barnett was taken over by Associated Motor Cycles (AMC), and it later abandoned Villiers to build its own two-stroke engines. These were unreliable, partly due to poor assembly. Fanny-B returned to Villiers power, which had served the company well in trials and scrambles competition as well as on roadgoing machines. But by the early 1960s parent company AMC was in financial trouble. Francis-Barnett was merged with James, and by the time production ended in the mid-1960s the two marques were barely distinguishable.

SPECIFICATIONS	FRANCIS-BARNETT CRUISER (1936)
Engine	Air-cooled two-stroke single
Capacity	249cc (63 x 80mm)
Maximum power	8hp
Transmission	Four-speed, chain final drive
Frame	Steel cradle
Suspension	Pressed-steel girder fork front; rigid rear
Brakes	Drum front and rear
Weight	250lb (113kg) approx
Top speed	55mph (89km/h)

Greeves

Although Greeves built fewer than 20,000 bikes in total, the Essex firm packed plenty of success and incident into its 23 years' production life. Bert Greeves began in business after the Second World War by building powered invalid carriages known as Invacars, in collaboration with his wheelchair-bound cousin Derry Preston-Cobb.

Below: This 20T trials model from 1955 features rubber-in-torsion suspension.
Below left: The 25DC two-stroke twin from 1963 was a typical post-war Greeves.

GREEVES HAD been a Norton owner and keen off-road rider before the war, and in the early 1950s designed and built a prototype scrambles (motocross) bike.

The first Greeves production bikes, 197cc and 242cc two-stroke roadsters plus a scrambler model, were launched in 1954. The roadsters combined bought-in engines, from Villiers and British Anzani, with innovative chassis. Their frames consisted of a single cast aluminium beam; and suspension front and rear was by rubber-in-torsion (rubber bushes that twisted under load), like the system fitted to the invalid carriages.

Greeves' roadsters earned a reputation for fine handling, but they sold in fairly small numbers and the firm's real success was with its competition machines. Dave Bickers' giant-killing victory in the 250cc European motocross championship in 1960 and '61 led to the successful Hawkstone production machine, and in 1964 Greeves introduced the Challenger model powered by a 360cc engine of its own construction. Greeves was also successful in trials and, with the Silverstone model, in club-level road-racing.

Through the late 1950s and 1960s the firm's road bike range

remained based around 250cc and 350cc twins, with names including Fleetmaster, Fleetwing and Sports Twin. The Essex twin was sold in modest numbers to police forces in the mid-1960s. But Japanese competition and the non-availability of Villiers engines halted Greeves roadster production shortly afterwards. And although the firm continued production of the Griffon off-roader into the 1970s, the end came when Bert Greeves and Derry Preston-Cobb retired in 1977.

SPECIFICATIONS	GREEVES 25DC SPORTS TWIN (1963)
Engine	Air-cooled two-stroke parallel twin
Capacity	249cc (50 x 63.5mm)
Maximum power	15bhp approx
Transmission	Four-speed, chain final drive
Frame	Aluminium downtube
Suspension	Rubber-in-torsion front; twin shocks rear
Brakes	Drum front and rear
Weight	270lb (122kg)
Top speed	70mph (113km/h)

Harris

In recent years Harris Performance has been best known for its road-racing connections with Japanese factories, notably in running Suzuki's World Superbike team and producing a chassis that enabled privateer riders to use Yamaha works engines in 500cc grands prix.

*B*UT THE firm from Hertford, run by brothers Lester and Steve Harris and partner Steve Bayford, has also produced a number of successful roadgoing sports machines powered by a variety of engines.

Ironically Harris's most significant all-British machine was produced by Triumph triple specialist Norman Hyde, and marketed under the name Hyde Harrier. This combined either a Triumph twin- or, more commonly, three-cylinder engine with a Harris-built, tubular-steel frame loosely based on the famous Rob North racing chassis. The top specification Harrier, with a racy fairing, high-quality cycle parts and a hotted-up Trident triple motor, was a fast and charismatic sportster.

The best known Harris roadsters were the Magnum café-racers, beginning with the Magnum 1, essentially a road-legal version of the British firm's Kawasaki Z1000-engined racebike of the late 1970s. A 1981 restyle by Target Design (creators of Suzuki's Katana) produced the Magnum 2, powered by the Z1000 and also, more commonly, by Suzuki's GSX1100 four. Over 800 of these fast and fine-handling roadburners were sold, despite their inevitably high price.

The Magnum 3, initially based on Kawasaki's GPz1100 engine, had a frame of steel tube and aluminum plate, plus rising-rate suspension and radical geometry compared to Japanese roadsters. Only a small number were built but the steel-framed Magnum 4, built around Suzuki's GSX-R750 and 1100 motors, was more handsome and successful. In 1996 Harris revised and restyled it to produce the Magnum 5, powered by the 16-valve engine from Honda's CBR900RR FireBlade.

SPECIFICATIONS	HARRIS/HYDE HARRIER (1990)
Engine	Air-cooled ohv six-valve triple
Capacity	973cc (71 x 82mm)
Maximum power	85bhp @ 7000rpm
Transmission	Five-speed, chain final drive
Frame	Steel twin downtube
Suspension	Telescopic front; twin shocks rear
Brakes	Twin disc front; single disc rear
Weight	380lb (172kg)
Top speed	135mph (217km/h)

Above right: Excellent suspension and a rigid Harris-built frame of Reynolds 531 steel tubing meant the Hyde Harrier handled well.

Right: The Harrier was generally produced with a 750cc three-cylinder Triumph Trident motor, but Harris had designed the chassis so that it would also take Triumph's twin-pot Bonneville motor.

Healey

The brief history of Healey motorcycles is essentially a short postscript to the long-drawn-out tale of the Ariel Square Four, production of which ended in 1958. Brothers George and Tim Healey were 'Squariel' enthusiasts who had competed in sprint races on modified machines during the 1960s.

Below: Healey's debt to Ariel can be clearly seen in the distinctive Square Four engine. This early model has drum brakes; later machines used discs.

THE BROTHERS then began producing spares for the bikes, and built up what was reportedly the world's largest stock of parts for the aluminium-engined Square Four 4G models.

In 1973 the Healeys took the plunge and went into business producing a bike of their own, based on the Square Four 4G Mk II engine. They improved the powerplant in various ways, mainly in respect of its lubrication: fitting an uprated oil pump and larger-capacity oil filter, and adding an oil-cooler. Peak power was a claimed 45bhp, later raised to 52bhp at 6000rpm by camshaft tuning. They first raised the compression ratio, then lowered it again to 7.5:1 to reduce harshness.

The bike's chassis was based on a frame designed by leading Swiss engineer Fritz Egli, and used his trademark layout of a large steel spine that doubled as the oil tank. Egli Vincent builder Roger Slater built the Healey frames, which held twin shocks and were initially equipped with front forks from Metal Profiles. Later models used Spanish-made Betor forks and Lockheed disc brakes.

The Healey 1000/4 was a handsome machine with a very respectable top speed of 120mph (193km/h) in its final form. It weighed a

SPECIFICATIONS	HEALEY 1000/4 (1977)
Engine	Air-cooled ohv eight-valve square-four
Capacity	997cc (65 x 75mm)
Maximum power	52bhp @ 6000rpm
Transmission	Four-speed, chain final drive
Frame	Steel spine
Suspension	Telescopic front; twin shocks rear
Brakes	Disc front; drum rear
Weight	380lb (172kg)
Top speed	120mph (193km/h)

competitive 380lb (172kg) and reportedly handled superbly. But in 1977 the Healey cost almost £2000 when, for example, Honda's ultra-sophisticated Gold Wing tourer cost only £1600. Perhaps inevitably, production came to an end when fewer than 20 bikes had been built.

Hesketh

When the Hesketh V1000 was revealed at Lord Alexander Hesketh's palatial Northamptonshire mansion in 1980, the big V-twin was introduced as a new British world-beater: a handsome, powerful, comfortable and fine-handling thoroughbred of a quality that was second to none.

Below and below left: With its bikini fairing and nickel-plated frame, the V1000 was a stylish machine but lacked the reliability to match.

*S*ADLY FOR his Lordship, who had previously owned a successful Formula One car racing team, that's not quite how it worked out. Instead the V1000 was plagued by faults that quickly led Hesketh into financial trouble.

The air-cooled motor was designed and built by Weslake, well-known engine consultants and producers of a successful single-cylinder speedway engine. Like that motor, the 992cc Hesketh V-twin featured twin overhead cams and four valves per cylinder. Peak output was 86bhp at 6500rpm, with a five-speed gearbox and chain final drive. The chassis was of high quality, combining a tubular steel frame with Marzocchi suspension and Brembo brakes from Italy.

Performance was in many respects good, as the Hesketh produced plenty of smooth, low-down torque and cruised effortlessly at speed, its rider partially sheltered by the small bikini fairing. Top speed was a slightly disappointing 120mph (193km/h). But the V1000's handling was excellent and its triple discs produced plenty of stopping power, although the bike was rather heavy. As a long-legged and comfortable sports-tourer the Hesketh could have been a genuine success.

That did not happen because the hand-built bike's high price did not prevent it developing a long list of mechanical problems. Its motor ran roughly at low speed and leaked oil, the clutch and rear chain gave trouble, and the gearbox was poor. The factory's output fell dramatically as its emphasis shifted to warranty work, and only 149 bikes had been produced when the firm went bust in 1982. Lord Hesketh formed a new company and introduced a faired tourer, the Vampire, but fewer than 50 were built before production once again ground to a halt.

SPECIFICATIONS	HESKETH V1000 (1982)
Engine	Air-cooled dohc, eight-valve 90-degree V-twin
Capacity	992cc (95 x 70mm)
Maximum power	86bhp @ 6500rpm
Transmission	Five-speed, chain final drive
Frame	Tubular steel
Suspension	Telescopic front; twin shock rear
Brakes	Disc front and rear
Weight	506lb (230kg)
Top speed	120mph (193km/h)

James

The motorcycles built by James in its latter years were small-capacity two-strokes, and the Birmingham marque's name carries none of the glamour popularly associated with the likes of Triumph or Norton. Yet James was one of the oldest of British manufacturers, and in its earlier years had built not only two-strokes but a variety of four-stroke singles and large V-twins.

Below left: Like most later James models, this 1962-model 250cc Superswift used Villiers power.

Below right: James had success in the 1920s with four-strokes such as this 350SS.

*L*IKE SO many older marques, James started as a bicycle manufacturer. Harry James began making pedal cycles in 1880, and in 1902 added a Belgian-made Minerva engine to produce the firm's first powered machine. ('James Cycle Co' would remain its name throughout.) By 1909 James had developed its own engine to power an innovative – though unsuccessful – machine featuring single-sided stub axles and drum brakes.

Production was hit by a factory fire shortly after the First World War, but James built a strong reputation during the 1920s, notably with its four-stroke V-twins. In the economically depressed 1930s James switched production to two-strokes. Powerplants were built in-house – James had taken over engine maker F.E. Baker in 1931 – or bought in from Villiers.

Villiers-engined bikes dominated post-war production although, like Francis-Barnett, the firm was taken over by AMC in 1947 and briefly used its own poorly-built motors. James two-strokes, including the 150cc Cadet, 200cc Captain plus the 250cc Commodore and Superswift models, were regarded as competent if

unremarkable machines. In latter years some were almost indistinguishable from those of AMC stablemate Francis-Barnett.

James' concentration on lightweights made the firm particularly vulnerable to competition from Japan, and the inevitable end came with AMC's collapse in 1966. Ironically in the last few years part of the James works was used as the headquarters for the fledgling Suzuki (GB) Ltd – who at least had the decency to use the back door and a different address...

SPECIFICATIONS	JAMES M25 SUPERSWIFT (1962)
Engine	Air-cooled two-stroke parallel twin
Capacity	249cc (66 x 73mm)
Maximum power	15bhp
Transmission	Four-speed, chain final drive
Frame	Steel cradle
Suspension	Telescopic front; twin shock rear
Brakes	Drum front and rear
Weight	300lb (136kg)
Top speed	70mph (113km/h)

Levis

The first Levis motorcycle, built by the Butterfield family of Birmingham in 1911, had a single-cylinder two-stroke engine of 211cc capacity. It was this same format, refined slightly in following years, that would introduce a great number of people in Britain to the pleasure of motorcycling.

Below left: A Levis rider and 1921 Popular on the annual Banbury Run.

Below right: Levis uprated the stroker single with increased capacity of 247cc.

*T*HE LEVIS Popular or 'Pop' was simple and cheap – under £50 in 1918 – and it had the advantage that it had separate petrol and oil tanks, instead of relying on petroil lubrication like many rivals.

Performance of the BSA Bantam or Yamaha FS1-E of its day was hardly guaranteed to get the novice rider excited – though the rudimentary braking system and the bike's inability to out-accelerate a barking dog occasionally did. The Levis Pop required paddling along to make it start, featured direct drive to the rear wheel by belt, and had a cruising speed of about 30mph (48km/h). It would negotiate quite steep hills at half that speed, but sometimes needed more paddling or even required the rider to dismount and run alongside to get to the top.

Motorcyclists' demand for greater sophistication eventually killed the Levis Pop. The firm introduced firstly a two-speed and then a three-speed gearbox, with chain drive instead of the belt. Capacity went up to 247cc, weight also increased, and crucially so did the price – until the little Levis found itself unable to compete with similarly priced four-strokes.

SPECIFICATIONS	LEVIS POPULAR (1921)
Engine	Air-cooled two-stroke single
Capacity	211cc (62 x 70mm)
Maximum power	Not known
Transmission	Direct belt drive
Frame	Steel diamond
Suspension	Girder forks; rigid rear
Brakes	Stirrup front; rim rear
Weight	120lb (54kg)
Top speed	35mph (56km/h)

Levis itself built its first four-stroke, an overhead-valve 346cc single, in 1927, and went on to generate a loyal following among owners who appreciated the bikes' almost handbuilt quality and vintage-style constant-loss lubrication system. The firm also continued to build two-strokes while introducing models including a 250cc overhead-camshaft single in 1933. But Levis abandoned bikes to build compressors when the Second World War began in 1939, and two-wheeled production was never resumed.

Matchless

Success came quickly to the Matchless marque, which was founded by the Collier family at Plumstead in south London in 1899. Brothers Charlie and Harry Collier were leading racers and in 1907, just five years after the firm's first machine had been built, Charlie won the single-cylinder race at the first-ever Isle of Man TT.

Below: Matchless's 500cc G80 was almost identical to the AJS Model 18.

Opposite top: The G50 single was basically a 500cc version of the AJS 7R.

Opposite below: The G12, a 650cc twin, was introduced in 1959.

*H*E AVERAGED 38.22mph (61.5km/h) over the 158-mile (254km) course on a JAP-engined Matchless. The winning bike was displayed on the firm's stand at that year's Motor Cycle Show, and a production version – one of the first race-replicas – was added to the range for the next year.

By this time Matchless had produced a variety of roadgoing models, notably a 1905 JAP-engined V-twin that incorporated the advanced features of swinging-arm rear suspension and leading-link forks. This and other models sold well, but it was through racing that Matchless continued to make its name. Harry Collier followed his brother's example by winning the TT in 1909, at a record speed

of 49.01mph (78.87km/h), and Charlie won again at a faster-still average speed in the following year.

Singles formed the basis of Matchless roadster production in those early years, but the firm was also well-known for its large-capacity V-twins. Matchless engines were highly regarded, and were also supplied to other firms including Coventry Eagle, OEC and even Brough Superior, as well as the Morgan car company.

In 1931 Matchless took over AJS, and moved its production from the Midlands down to Plumstead. That same year the firm launched the unconventional Silver Arrow, a 400cc V-twin designed by Charlie Collier. But its 50mph (80km/h) performance was

mediocre and sales poor. Two years later, younger brother Bert produced the Silver Hawk, with a more powerful 600cc V4 engine that was essentially two Arrow units side-by-side. The motor was noisy and prone to oil leaks. The Silver Hawk was also expensive, and the model was dropped after only 500 had been built.

Matchless was more successful with simpler single-cylinder models. Among the best was the 350cc ohv G3 that was launched in 1935 as the Clubman, and later modified to form the G3L that was produced for military use in the Second World War. In 1941 Matchless made a major advance with the introduction of its telescopic, hydraulically damped front forks, which were patented under the name Teledraulic. The G3L became even more popular with army despatch riders, and was later adapted for civilian use in models such as the G3LS of 1959.

The best-known competition Matchless was the G50 single, essentially a 500cc version of the 350cc AJS 7R. The G50 was first

produced in 1959, by which time the era of single-cylinder dominance in grands prix had ended. But the Matchless proved a worthy rival to Norton's Manx. Although slightly less powerful, producing about 50bhp, the G50 was lighter. It became popular as an over-the-counter racer, partly because it was relatively inexpensive and easy to maintain.

AMC suffered financial problems and went bust in 1966, after which rights to G50 production were bought by former racer and engineer Colin Seeley, who continued engine development and also built his own chassis to create the Seeley G50. The four-stroke single G50 held its own against the two-strokes until the 1970s, and in recent years has been competitive in classic racing. Given the dramatic way in which Matchless began its racing career, it's ironic that when American Dave Roper won the Historic TT in 1984, it was the marque's first TT win since co-founder Charlie Collier's victory back in 1910.

SPECIFICATIONS	MATCHLESS G50 (1961)
Engine	Air-cooled two-valve sohc single
Capacity	496cc (90 x 78mm)
Maximum power	51bhp @ 7200rpm
Transmission	Four-speed, chain final drive
Frame	Steel cradle
Suspension	Telescopic front; twin shock rear
Brakes	Drum front and rear
Weight	290lb (132kg)
Top speed	135mph (217km/h)

New Hudson

The prefix 'New' was used by a dozen or more firms during the early 1920s, and although New Hudson ceased production in 1933 it was more successful than most. (By way of comparison, the New Comet, New Era, New Knight, New Paragon and New Ryder failed to see out the decade.)

*I*N TYPICAL fashion the firm had its roots in bicycle production in the 1890s, and began fitting some of its bicycles with single-cylinder Minerva engines from Belgium in the early years of the 20th century.

By 1910 New Hudson was producing proper motorcycles, and in 1911 began using its own engine, a 499cc side-valve single. Later models were powered by 350cc singles and 700cc side-valve V-twins, and in 1914 New Hudson introduced a 211cc single-cylinder two-stroke whose engine resembled that of the popular Levis.

The firm produced overhead-valve four-strokes from the mid-1920s, and in 1931 introduced a range of handsome 346cc and 493cc models whose engines featured partial enclosure with casings around their crankcases and primary transmission. Models including the Bronze Wing and the 493cc Model 3 had angled-forward single cylinders with enclosed valvegear and four-speed gearboxes by Moss or Burman.

New Hudson specification also included tank-top instruments and touring fitments ranging from legshields to 'travelling suitcases'. But the bike-buying public was unconvinced, and in 1933 the firm abandoned the manufacture of motorcycles to build suspension and brake parts for Girling.

In 1940 New Hudson returned to two wheels with an autocycle, powered by a 98cc Villiers two-stroke engine. It provided cheap wartime transport and was also produced after the war, by which time manufacturing rights had been sold to BSA. It was gradually updated, gaining girder forks, engine shields, a new frame and updated engine, until production ended in 1958.

SPECIFICATIONS	NEW HUDSON MODEL 3 (1932)
Engine	Air-cooled ohc two-valve single
Capacity	493cc
Maximum power	Not known
Transmission	Four-speed, chain final drive
Frame	Steel cradle
Suspension	Girder front; rigid rear
Brakes	Drum front and rear
Weight	Not known
Top speed	65mph (105km/h) approx

Above right: This 500cc overhead-valve single dates from 1932, the year after New Hudson introduced a range of four-strokes with partially enclosed bottom-ends.

Right: After beginning engine manufacture with a side-valve single, New Hudson moved on to pushrod singles in the mid-1920s, and built this 500cc model in 1929.

New Imperial

Alongside many simple single-cylinder roadsters, Birmingham firm New Imperial made its mark with the production of technically advanced roadsters and a string of rapid racers and record-breakers.

Below: This 500cc New Imperial single dates from 1938, one of the firm's last years of production, and features the Birmingham marque's new Vincent-style cantilever rear suspension system.

THE FIRM began in 1901 with an unsuccessful machine that located its 500cc engine above the front wheel. Production was restarted in 1910, with a more conventional bike fitted with a 292cc side-valve single engine from JAP, who continued to provide both singles and V-twins into the 1920s.

New Imperial's first major sporting triumph came in 1924, when Eddie Twemlow won the Junior and Lightweight TTs. Further TT glory followed in the 1930s, with Leo Davenport's Lightweight win in 1932 and Bob 'Fearless' Foster's remarkable victory by over five minutes in the same event four years later.

The firm's record-breaking exploits were no less notable, headed by Ginger Wood's achievement at Brooklands in 1934, when he became the first rider of a British multi-cylinder machine to cover over 100 miles (161km) in an hour. Wood's New Imp V-twin wobbled horribly over the bumps on the banked track during the run, but a year later he brought the firm more prestige by raising the lap record to 115.82mph (186.4km/h).

New Imperial had been building its own engines since 1926, and six years later launched its first machine featuring the novelty of a unit-construction engine and gearbox. The basic model was the Unit Minor 150, which took advantage of the lower rate of road tax for sub-150cc machines. It was followed by the Unit Super 250, Unit Plus 350 and Unit Major 500.

By 1938 almost the whole of New Imperial's 20-bike range was unit-construction, and some also boasted a Vincent-style rear suspension system. But shortly afterwards the firm was bought by Jack Sangster, owner of Ariel and Triumph, and production did not restart after the end of the Second World War.

SPECIFICATIONS	NEW IMPERIAL MODEL 110 (1939)
Engine	Air-cooled ohv four-valve single
Capacity	496cc (82 x 94mm)
Maximum power	Not known
Transmission	Four-speed, chain final drive
Frame	Steel cradle
Suspension	Girder front; triangulated spring rear
Brakes	Drum front and rear
Weight	Not known
Top speed	80mph (129km/h)

Norton International

James Lansdowne Norton began by making spares for the bicycle trade in Birmingham in 1898, and progressed to building his first motorcycle four years later. More than 100 years after the firm was founded, its decades of competition glory and the many fine roadsters produced over the years ensure that Norton remains one of the greatest names in motorcycling.

Below: With its large-capacity petrol tank and Amal TT carburettor, Norton's International was basically a roadgoing version of the firm's works racebikes, and had unbeatable performance in the 1930s.

*R*ACING SUCCESS gave the struggling Norton company an early boost when, in 1907, Rem Fowler won the twin-cylinder class of the first Isle of Man TT. James Norton was encouraged, and a year later began production of single- and twin-cylinder bikes using engines of his own construction. Early models included the 490cc 16H, a high-performance roadster, and the 633cc long-stroke Big 4, which was named after its 4hp rating and was popular for pulling sidecars.

James Norton himself competed in the TT between 1909 and 1911, retiring on each occasion. He later became unwell, having suffered from a heart condition for some time. His business became run-down during his long convalescence, eventually going into liquidation in 1913. But the company was revived shortly afterwards as Norton Motors Ltd, under the joint directorship of Norton and Bob Shelley, whose brother-in-law Dan 'Wizard' O'Donovan was a top racer and tuner.

Norton's First TT Victory

The first of Norton's many TT wins came in the very first event, in 1907, when Rem Fowler won the twin-cylinder race on a Peugeot-engined machine he had bought direct from the works. Fowler averaged 36.22mph (58.29km/h) to win the ten-lap, 158-mile (254km) race, but he did not have an easy time. At one stage he had lost so much time changing spark plugs, tyres and drive belts that he decided to retire, only to be told by a spectator that he was leading by half an hour. His winning machine is now one of the many Nortons on display in the National Motorcycle Museum in Birmingham.

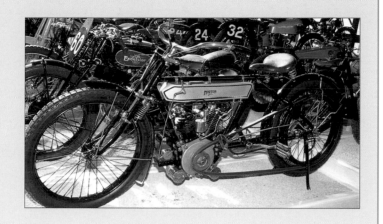

O'Donovan was based at Brooklands, and developed the 490cc Norton single to produce the Brooklands Special or BS. The bike was sold with a certificate confirming that it had exceeded 75mph (121km/h) at the Surrey track. The BS was arguably the world's first production racing bike, and was also built in Brooklands Road Special (BRS) form, timed at 70mph (113km/h). The chassis that O'Donovan used to test the BS and BRS engines at Brooklands was later restored to form the basis of 'Old Miracle', star of many classic events over the years.

In 1922 Norton converted the side-valve single engine to overhead-valve operation, producing the Model 18 roadster. The bottom half of its engine was almost identical to that of the Model H side-valve unit, but valve operation was now by pushrods and rockers. The ohv single won the Senior TT in 1924 but tragedy struck Norton a year later when 'Pa' Norton, whose heart condition had worsened, died at the age of 56.

Norton's last big technical advance of the 1920s came with the launch of the overhead-cam CS1 – short for Cam Shaft Mk 1 – in 1927. Designed by Walter Moore, who later produced a similar

layout for NSU, the 490cc CS1 combined its bevel-driven overhead cam engine with a new cradle frame plus girder forks. The CS1 rapidly became successful in racing, being ridden to victory by the great Stanley Woods and others, and was released as a super-sports roadster in 1928.

In 1932 Norton again uprated the single with the International model, which featured a revised engine of 350cc or 500cc. The 'Inter' was essentially a roadgoing version of Norton's works racers. It came with an Amal TT carburettor, four-speed gearbox and large-capacity petrol tank, and was the fastest and most glamorous sports machine of its day.

SPECIFICATIONS	NORTON INTERNATIONAL (1932)
Engine	Air-cooled ohv two-valve single
Capacity	490cc (79 x 100mm)
Maximum power	29bhp @ 5500rpm
Transmission	Four-speed, chain final drive
Frame	Steel cradle
Suspension	Girder front; rigid rear
Brakes	Drum front and rear
Weight	355lb (161kg)
Top speed	90mph (145km/h)

Above: Rem Fowler's 1907 TT-winner now resides in the National Motorcycle Museum, Birmingham.
Left: The CS1, introduced as a sporting roadster in 1928, featured a 490cc single engine with bevel drive to single overhead cam, and a new chassis with girder forks.

Norton Manx

Several decades of development helped to make the Manx Norton one of the most successful racing bikes of all time. The overhead-camshaft single's simplicity and its remarkable performance, confirmed by countless race victories all over the world – often against more powerful multi-cylinder opposition – not only made the Manx hugely popular, but gave the Norton marque an aura of quality that benefited even the humblest model of the range.

Below and opposite below: The single-cylinder simplicity of the Manx Norton is clear in this immaculate 500cc Manx 30M, which is not an original bike but a new Norton built for classic racing by model specialist Bernie Allen.

THE FIRST true Manx models combined Norton's single-cylinder engine with the single-tube 'Garden Gate' frame, fitted with plunger rear suspension. (Pre-war customer racebikes had shared the name International with the roadsters to which they were closely related.) The engine was uprated to twin-camshaft specification on the works racers in 1937.

In 1950, following an unsuccessful 1949 season, Norton factory race manager Joe Craig fitted the team's bikes with an innovative chassis designed by Irish racer/engineer Rex McCandless. Its twin-loop cradle design gave much improved handling under racing conditions, and also proved stronger and easier to manufacture.

Works rider Harold Daniell unwittingly christened the frame when he commented that the new bike felt like riding a feather bed. The new bike made a sensational debut when Norton took the first three places in both Senior and Junior TTs. In future years the Featherbed Manx was offered for general sale. It was produced in

Classic Racing

The Manx Norton story gained an unexpected new chapter in 1992 when, after a gap of 30 years, the motorcycle entered production once again. The model's success in the fast-growing classic racing scene in the 1980s had led many firms to produce new components, ranging from complete engines and frames to small details. Realizing that all the parts existed to build a new Manx, restorer and former racer Bernie Allen began production of a small series of bikes.

Allen's engine was precisely as delivered by Norton in 1961, apart from one washer made unnecessary by modern machining methods. So too were the Featherbed frame and Roadholder forks. Allen added period parts including twin Armstrong shocks, 19-inch alloy wheels and a magnesium front drum brake. The resultant bikes helped keep the Manx to the fore in classic racing, often competing with replica Matchless G50s built in similar fashion by George Beale.

Above: The 350cc Manx 40M was less successful than the bigger model, but still won many races over the years.

both 500cc and 350cc capacities, with the larger model being known as the 30M and the smaller the 40M.

Although the 500cc Manx was the more successful, both models recorded hundreds of victories worldwide. The Manx established itself as the archetypal single-cylinder racer. Its lean, simple look was built around the heavily-finned engine, Featherbed frame, a large silver tank with black pinstriping, clip-on handlebars, small flyscreen and Roadholder forks. The megaphone exhaust was often flattened to increase ground clearance.

Geoff Duke gave the Manx its finest moments, winning both the 500cc and 350cc world championships in 1951, and retaining the 350 title in '52. But the era of single-cylinder supremacy at grand prix level was drawing to a close. Duke left Norton to join Gilera of Italy, and won a further three titles on multi-cylinder machines. In 1954 Joe Craig introduced a new short-stroke engine design. But although this gave the single a new lease of life at privateer level, Norton would not win another world title.

Norton's factory team was disbanded in 1955, but the Manx continued to be built for sale until 1962, and remained successful competitively thanks partly to the efforts of tuners including Steve Lancefield and Ray Petty. Mike Hailwood scored a final TT victory for the single in 1961, and a Norton ridden by Godfrey Nash won the Yugoslavian GP as late as 1969. But Yamaha's two-stroke twins took over in the 1970s, and the glory days of the Manx looked to be over.

SPECIFICATIONS	NORTON MANX 30M (1962)
Engine	Air-cooled dohc two-valve single
Capacity	498cc (86 x 85.8mm)
Maximum power	50bhp @ 7000rpm
Transmission	Four-speed, chain final drive
Frame	Steel twin cradle Featherbed
Suspension	Roadholder telescopic front; twin shock rear
Brakes	Drum front and rear
Weight	309lb (140kg)
Top speed	140mph (225km/h)

Norton Dominator

Norton introduced the 500cc parallel twin Dominator in 1949, to compete with Triumph's Speed Twin, which had been a huge success since its introduction in 1938. The 29bhp motor of the original Dominator Model 7 was designed by Bert Hopwood, who had worked at both Ariel and Triumph with Edward Turner and who had been responsible for putting many of Turner's ideas into practice.

*H*OPWOOD HAD left Norton by the time the Model 7 reached production. But his twin-cylinder engine design, with a single camshaft positioned in front of the cylinders, would serve the company for well over two decades. The Model 7 had a plunger frame similar to that of Norton's single-cylinder ES2. Although it handled reasonably well, the bike was overshadowed a few years later by the Featherbed-framed Dominator 88, which was launched on the export market in 1952 and in Britain in '53.

The Featherbed had become famous because of its use on the single-cylinder racing Manx. But the revolutionary frame had been designed to house various types of Norton engine and gearbox, and its distinctive twin-loop design proved ideally suited to the twin-cylinder powerplant. The Dominator 88's improved handling, coupled with the fact that it was considerably lighter than the Model 7, made the 88 a big success.

Norton uprated both the engine and chassis through the 1950s. In 1955 the 88 engine gained an alloy cylinder head, higher compression and an Amal Monobloc carburettor, while the rear subframe was welded on, rather than bolted, and held a revised dual-seat. A year later came the Dominator 99, with its engine bored and stroked to increase capacity to 600cc. Like the 88, it was fitted with a race-developed Daytona camshaft that helped lift top speed to just over 100mph (161km/h).

In 1960 Norton introduced the slimline Featherbed frame, complete with new rear subframe and narrower fuel tank, whose smaller dimensions made for a more manageable bike. And two years later came perhaps the finest twin of all, the 650SS Dominator, when this excellent chassis was fitted with an enlarged, long-stroke 646cc motor whose high-compression alloy cylinder head and pair of Amal carburettors helped boost peak output to an impressive 49bhp at 6800rpm.

The 650SS (standing for Sports Special) roared to a top speed of 115mph (185km/h) yet was reasonably smooth, and its handling lived up to Norton's advertising line 'the world's best road holder'.

Right: The Dominator 88's styling was understated, but few bikes of the 1950s and early 1960s could match the 500cc twin's blend of smooth performance and fine handling.

Opposite below: In 1960 Norton uprated the Dominator with the Slimline Featherbed frame, which was more compact and easier to handle while retaining the 88's power delivery and stability. The similarly styled 650SS of 1962 added more power and speed.

Triumph's recently released Bonneville was slightly faster, but the 650SS was a match for any bike in the bends, as a string of impressive production race performances confirmed.

The 650cc twins – there were also Standard and de Luxe versions with softer engines – were reasonably successful, and helped Norton gain a foothold in the capacity-hungry American export market. But when the engine was bored out from 68 to 73mm to produce the 745cc Atlas, the resultant high level of vibration quickly made it clear that the capacity limit of the solidly mounted parallel twin had been exceeded.

By this time Norton had even more important things to worry about. In 1962 Associated Motor Cycles (AMC), which had taken over Norton nine years earlier, had announced that production at Norton's famous Bracebridge Street factory in Birmingham would close. The Atlas was the last model to be built there before production was switched to Woolwich in south London, where Norton was amalgamated with Matchless.

For the next few years Norton and Matchless models became increasingly similar, in many cases almost identical. But the confusion lasted only until 1966, when AMC's financial problems deepened and the receiver was called in. AMC marques Matchless, James and Francis-Barnett perished, but Norton was taken over by Manganese Bronze Holdings, and remained in business.

SPECIFICATIONS	NORTON DOMINATOR 88 (1960)
Engine	Air-cooled ohv four-valve parallel twin
Capacity	497cc (66 x 73mm)
Maximum power	30bhp @ 7000rpm
Transmission	Four-speed, chain final drive
Frame	Steel twin cradle Featherbed
Suspension	Roadholder telescopic front; twin shocks rear
Brakes	Drum front and rear
Weight	405lb (184kg)
Top speed	95mph (153km/h)

Norton Commando

Norton created the Commando in 1967 by combining a 745cc parallel twin engine with a new chassis that used innovative Isolastic rubber mounts to reduce the vibration passed to the rider. Striking styling – especially in the early form that earned it the Fastback name – plus fine handling helped make the Commando a big hit.

Below: Early Fastback-styled 750 Commandos were fast and fine-handling machines with minimal vibration thanks to Norton's Isolastic system.
Opposite: Upping the Commando's capacity to 828cc increased torque and helped make the large-tanked Interstate a practical tourer.

THE COMMANDO confirmed its status as one of the best and most popular bikes of the late 1960s and early '70s by winning the *Motor Cycle News* Machine of the Year competition five years in a row.

The Commando made an immediate impact when unveiled at the Earls Court Show in 1967. As well as its distinctive long fibreglass seat unit, the bike was finished in silver and had no Norton name on its tank, though production machines were more traditionally finished when they appeared early in 1968. The engine was heavily based on the Atlas unit, but it was angled forward in the chassis, and produced a maximum of 58bhp at 6800rpm.

But it was the patented Isolastic engine-mounting system, developed by a team headed by former Rolls-Royce engineer Dr Stefan Bauer, that was the Commando's most important innovation. The frame consisted of a large main spine plus twin downtubes, to which the engine was attached by means of rubber mounts. Rear engine plates were similarly rubber-mounted, isolating the power unit while leaving the large frame spine to resist torsional stresses.

The design was a success on two counts. It made the parallel twin engine feel remarkably smooth, allowing the rider to take full advantage of its generous mid-range torque and 115mph (185km/h) top speed. And the Commando also maintained

Norton's reputation for fine handling, aided in this respect by efficient Roadholder front forks.

Norton introduced various updates and spin-off models during the next few years, some of them short-lived. The Commando SS was a 1971-model street scrambler with a small fuel tank and high-level exhausts, aimed at the American market. The Commando Hi-Rider combined a similar tank with high handlebars and a chopper-style seat.

The fastest but most troublesome variant was the Combat Commando, a high-performance machine with flatter handlebars, new pipes and a tuned motor producing 65bhp. One of the ways that the extra 5bhp had been found was by increasing the compression ratio, but the main bearings had not been sufficiently

uprated to suit that development. Warranty claims soon began to flood in. Attempts to rectify the situation by lowering compression using a new aluminium head gasket merely added to Norton's problems, when this began to leak.

In 1973 Norton bored-out the standard model's 745cc engine to produce the 850 Commando, which was available in standard Roadster and large-tanked Interstate versions. The 828cc unit was torquey and reliable, but Norton's attempts to update it with an electric starter two years later, on the Commando Mk III, were less successful. By now the British twin was showing its age in comparison with newer designs, especially those from Japan.

Commando production eventually ended in 1977, when parent company Norton Villiers Triumph went into liquidation. But components continue to be made, and in recent years Midlands parts specialist Fair Spares has used these to build small numbers of 'new' Commandos, identical to the originals.

Racing Success

Despite lacking power when compared to most of its circuit rivals, the Commando was raced with success in the early Seventies. Norton's Formula 750 racer used an innovative steel monocoque frame that enjoyed advantages in terms of weight and aerodynamics. The bike was developed and ridden by Peter Williams, who won the 1973 Formula 750 TT on it. Another notable racebike was the Cosworth Challenge, a 750cc vertical twin whose engine was essentially two cylinders taken from Cosworth Engineering's liquid-cooled 3-litre V8 Formula One car engine. Lack of funds prevented the 95bhp Challenge from realizing its full potential.

SPECIFICATIONS	NORTON COMMANDO (1968)
Engine	Air-cooled ohv four-valve parallel twin
Capacity	745cc (73 x 89mm)
Maximum power	58bhp @ 6800rpm
Transmission	Four-speed, chain final drive
Frame	Steel spine with twin downtubes
Suspension	Telescopic front; twin shock rear
Brakes	Drum front and rear
Weight	420lb (190kg)
Top speed	115mph (185km/h)

Norton F1

A new era dawned for Norton in 1987 with the appearance of the 588cc rotary-engined Classic, the result of more than 15 years of slow, low-budget development work that had seen rotary bikes used by several police forces. The Classic housed its 79bhp air-cooled, twin-chamber rotary engine in a competent, if dated, twin-shock chassis. It combined naked styling with 125mph (201km/h) top speed, ultra-smooth cruising and solid handling.

NORTON SOLD a limited run of 100 Classics and also developed a touring model, the Commander. After that promising start, interest took off when a handful of workers, led by engineer Brian Crighton, built an alloy-framed rotary racer whose performances were first encouraging, then astonishing. In 1989, ridden by Steve Spray, the fire-breathing, 135bhp rotary racer won two National championships, to the delight of huge crowds.

A roadgoing version was the obvious next step. The fully-faired F1 sportster, launched the following year, was powered by a Commander engine, turned back-to-front and fitted with the five-speed gearbox from Yamaha's FZR1000. Enlarged ports and revised timing helped lift output from 85bhp to 95bhp at 9500rpm. The aluminium frame, built by Spondon Engineering, was similar to that of the racebike. Dutch firm White Power provided the multi-adjustable upside-down forks and shock; Brembo brakes and Michelin radials completed an upmarket package.

SPECIFICATIONS	NORTON F1 (1990)
Engine	Liquid-cooled twin-chamber rotary
Capacity	588cc
Maximum power	91bhp @ 9500rpm
Transmission	Five-speed, chain final drive
Frame	Aluminium twin spar
Suspension	Telescopic front: single shock rear
Brakes	Twin disc front; single disc rear
Weight	422lb (191kg)
Top speed	145mph (233km/h)

The F1's power and weight figures were similar to those of a typical Japanese 600, and so was its 145mph (233km/h) top speed. On the road, the rotary felt totally different, though, thanks to its smoothness and distinctive exhaust note. For a sportster the F1 was fairly comfortable, and it handled well. But there were rough edges: the Norton was thirsty, its engine snatched at low revs and was prone to overheating, and ground clearance was poor.

The hand-built F1 was also extremely expensive, and only small numbers were sold. By the mid-1990s Norton's tentative business recovery had foundered, several former directors had been convicted of financial irregularities, and hundreds of enthusiast

shareholders had lost the money they had invested in the company. Rotary production was abandoned by the firm's new Canadian owners, and the Shenstone factory was left to produce only a small quantity of spare parts.

The Norton story burst into life again in 1998, the marque's centenary year, with two rival attempts at a production revival. The more spectacular – if less realistic – came from the firm's Canadian owners, the Aquilini family, in conjunction with March Motors of America and Lancashire-based engineering firm MCD, headed by Al Melling best known for work in the car industry.

At a launch at London's Dorchester Hotel, Norton Motors International unveiled a sleek prototype superbike named the Nemesis, which they claimed was powered by a 1500cc liquid-cooled V8 engine producing no less than 280bhp. With a top speed of 225mph (362km/h), the Nemesis would be far faster than any previous production motorcycle.

The exotic V8 also boasted advanced technical features including push-button gearchange and clutch, active suspension and perimeter rim disc brakes. Norton optimistically claimed that the Nemesis would be produced at Shenstone in six months' time. But even the prototype had not been seriously tested months after that, and Norton's hoped-for injection of cash had not materialized.

Meanwhile Joe Seifert, whose Norton Motors Deutschland firm owned rights to the Norton name in most of Europe, had begun low-volume production of a single-cylinder roadster called the C652SM. This combined the 652cc single-cylinder engine from BMW's F650 with a steel-framed chassis built by British specialist Tigcraft. Top speed was just over 100mph (161km/h), and the bike handled very well. Ironically Seifert did not own rights to the Norton name in Britain, so the C652SM could not be sold in Norton's traditional home market.

OEC

Often referred to as the 'Odd Engineering Company' because of its willingness to try something different, OEC was best known for its innovative duplex steering system. The first initial of the family firm's name in fact stood for Osborn. John Osborn, who had taken over from his father Frederick, designed the duplex system that was fitted to many of the OEC bikes that were produced in a succession of factories near Portsmouth on the south coast before the Second World War.

SPECIFICATIONS	OEC COMMANDER (1928)
Engine	Air-cooled ohv two-valve single
Capacity	498cc (82.5 x 93mm)
Maximum power	20bhp approx
Transmission	Four-speed, chain final drive
Frame	Steel cradle
Suspension	Duplex front; plunger rear
Brakes	Drum front and rear
Weight	300lb (136kg)
Top speed	80mph (129km/h)

THE HISTORY of OEC dates back to 1901, when the first bikes were built using Belgian-made Minerva engines. The OEC models produced in the early 1920s were identical to Blackburne bikes that actually died out in that period. OEC had previously assembled Blackburne bikes, and continued to use the old firm's engines, including an overhead-camshaft 350cc unit that powered a racing model.

In 1927 OEC introduced its first machine with the complex duplex steering system, which gave excellent stability at the expense of poor low-speed manoeuvrability and a huge turning circle. Duplex steering was fitted to a wide variety of powerplants from firms including Blackburne, JAP, Matchless, Python and Villiers; and in capacities ranging from 150 to 1000cc.

Among the best-known models was the Commander of 1938, which was powered by a 500cc Matchless single-cylinder motor and combined 80mph (129km/h) top speed with excellent stability. The OEC chassis also proved its worth in 1930 when a duplex-steering bike with a supercharged 1000cc JAP V-twin engine was timed at 137.32mph (220.95km/h) to set a new world speed record.

OEC production was halted by the Second World War but restarted in 1949, with conventional lightweight bikes powered by 122cc and 197cc Villiers two-stroke engines. Both machines were given the name Atlanta, and in 1951 they were joined by an Apollo model with a 248cc side-valve Brockhouse engine. None was particularly successful, and production ended in 1954.

Below: This 1938-model 500cc Commander features duplex steering.

OK Supreme

The name OK Supreme originated in 1927, when Ernie Humphries bought out his partner, Charles Dawes, from the family firm that had been building motorcycles since the turn of the century. Previously the firm had been called simply OK, and had produced a variety of models including Villiers- and Union-engined two-stroke lightweights, and four-strokes powered by motors from JAP, Bradshaw and Blackburne.

Below left: OK Supreme's overhead-cam works racing single acquired its nickname of "the Lighthouse" due to the glass window in its bevel-drive tower.

Below: Famous rider and tuner Bill Lacey tries out an OK Supreme at the banked Brooklands track.

*A*FTER DAWES had left to concentrate successfully on the bicycles with which the firm had entered production (under the name Humphries and Dawes) in 1882, racing fanatic Humphries aimed up-market. He was quickly rewarded when Frank Longman won the Lightweight TT in 1928, lapping at over 64mph (103km/h) on a JAP-engined bike fitted with a special cylinder head.

Two years later OK Supreme launched a 250cc overhead-cam single, the TT30, which gained the nickname 'Lighthouse' because of the glass window in the aluminium bevel-drive tower leading to its camshaft. The sports model was an attractive machine that was capable of 70mph (113km/h), and was quiet and reasonably oil-tight. Although sales of the 250 earned the company publicity, it cost too much to make to be profitable at the prices OK Supreme could charge.

Humphries' answer was the 250cc Dauntless, which was powered by a three-speed JAP single engine. To keep the price to a competitive £34, it was conservatively finished using enamel on the

handlebars, petrol tank and wheels, where other marques used chrome. In 1939 the firm introduced a 250cc side-valve utility bike, the SV/39, but few were sold before war broke out.

In 1946 Ernie's son John Humphries revived the OK Supreme name by building JAP-engined grass-track racers, but he was killed shortly afterwards and production did not continue.

SPECIFICATIONS	OK SUPREME DAUNTLESS (1935)
Engine	Air-cooled ohv two-valve single
Capacity	249cc (62.5 x 80mm)
Maximum power	Not known
Transmission	Three-speed, chain final drive
Frame	Steel cradle
Suspension	Girder front; rigid rear
Brakes	Drum front and rear
Weight	Not known
Top speed	60mph (97km/h)

P&M (Panther)

Few marques have been as closely associated with one type of motorcycle as Phelon & Moore, whose reputation for slow-revving 'sloper' singles lasted from the firm's foundation in 1904 to its demise more than 60 years later. The large-capacity Panther, as the bikes were known after 1923, was ideal for use with a sidecar thanks to its economy, reliability and generous low-rev pulling power.

OAH PHELON'S first prototype bike, which he built in 1900 at the engineering firm that he ran in Cleckheaton, South Yorkshire with Harry Rayner, featured just such a layout. The bike was notable for the innovative way in which its angled-forward cylinder was used as the frame's front downtube. Phelon sold production rights to Humber of Coventry (who paid a royalty of 7s 6d for each machine) but retained his patents, and continued to build machines in small numbers.

When Rayner was killed in a car crash, Phelon was approached by a steam engineer named Richard Moore, and the pair founded P&M in 1904. Their 500cc single initially sported an automatic inlet valve but was soon modified to side-valve layout, and also gained magneto ignition, a contracting-band rear brake and leading-link forks of the firm's own design.

In 1923 P&M hired Granville Bradshaw, famed designer of the ABC flat-twin. His new single, the first Panther model, caused a

Opposite top: P&M introduced the Panther name on its ohv sloper in 1923, and in later years it became synonymous with the marque.

Opposite below: This is the classical Panther scene: a 600cc sloper hitched to an enormous, fully-enclosed sidecar with room for all the family. The arrival of cheap small cars spelled the beginning of the end for P&M.

Right: Unlike the large Panthers, smaller-capacity machines such as this 250cc Model 70 from 1934 had a conventional frame downtube alongside a sloping single cylinder.

sensation at that year's Olympia Show. It retained the traditional P&M layout of using the engine as a frame member, but was an overhead-valve model with pushrods housed in a tube, and featured an alloy primary chaincase, new four-speed gearbox and a Dynamag combined ignition and electric lighting system.

The Panther's lively performance encouraged P&M to try its luck on the Isle of Man in 1924. The first attempt ended in farce when the two Panther riders collided, putting them out of the race. But Tommy Bullus' fourth place in the following year's Senior TT was impressive on what was essentially a standard roadster.

Bradshaw was less successful when in 1927 he tried a new approach with the Panthette. This was a 250cc transverse V-twin, and featured a unit-construction engine and gearbox, plus some other ingenious engineering. But its performance was mediocre,

and sales were very poor. P&M had built up a large supply of forged-steel frame members in readiness, and were forced to introduce a range of Villiers-engined two-strokes to use them up.

P&M hit further problems in the Depression-scarred 1930s with the 250cc Model 20, which combined a sloping single cylinder with a conventional front-downtube frame. In desperation the Yorkshire firm struck a deal with London dealer Pride & Clarke, who were able to sell the bargain-basement Red Panther model at just under £30. It was cheap but cheerful, and even won the Maudes Trophy in 1934.

After the Second World War the firm built various models including a two-stroke scooter, the Princess, but its mainstay remained the sloper singles. The best known was the Model 100, whose long-stroke 598cc engine had been introduced in 1928, and which remained in production with relatively few changes until 1963. The Model 120, launched in 1959, had a larger 645cc capacity, but still produced only 27bhp.

Both models gave slow-revving, undramatic, but efficient and fairly smooth performance – ideal for hitching to a big Busmar Astral sidecar for family transport. But P&M's reliance on the sidecar brigade – in 1960 the firm estimated that 90 per cent of Model 100s were attached to chairs – left it vulnerable when the attraction of three wheels began to fade. After a last fling with a stylish 250cc Villiers-engined two-stroke twin for which the Red Panther name was revived, the Cleckheaton factory closed in 1967.

SPECIFICATIONS	PANTHER MODEL 100 (1957)
Engine	Air-cooled ohv two-valve single
Capacity	598cc (87 x 100mm)
Maximum power	23bhp @ 5300rpm
Transmission	Four-speed, chain final drive
Frame	Steel spine
Suspension	Telescopic front; twin shock rear
Brakes	Drum front and rear
Weight	425lb (193kg)
Top speed	70mph (113km/h)

Quasar

The wedge-shaped Quasar, with its roof and feet-first riding position, was one of the most futuristic bikes ever produced in Britain, or indeed anywhere else. Introduced by Bristol-based duo Malcolm Newell and Ken Leaman in 1976, it was designed to provide motorcycling allied with the comfort and weather protection of a car.

Below left: The Quasar's aerodynamic shape gave it a higher top speed than a conventional bike of similar power.

Below right: Malcolm Newell made his name but no fortune with the innovative but ultimately unsuccessful Quasar.

*T*HE QUASAR'S striking bodywork was constructed from glass-fibre, mounted on a duplex frame of tubular steel that enclosed the whole machine to provide an element of crash-protection. The rider sat back on a hammock-like seat, and was treated to a heater and cassette player as well as a two-speed wiper for the long, sloping windscreen. The seat could be adjusted rearwards to make space for a rather cramped passenger.

Power was provided by the 848cc water-cooled four-cylinder engine from the Reliant three-wheeler. Peak output was 40bhp, feeble by 1970s superbike standards, but the softly-tuned pushrod unit suited the vehicle in having plenty of low-rev torque plus shaft final drive.

Despite its lack of power the Quasar was quite fast, with a top speed of about 100mph (161km/h), thanks largely to its aerodynamic efficiency. It was capable of cruising smoothly and effortlessly at 90mph (145km/h) or more. The bike also handled very well despite its long wheelbase and 690lb (313kg) of weight, and stopped hard thanks to triple disc brakes.

Sadly for its creators, the Quasar never sold in serious numbers, partly due to its high price (£3500 in 1976, when BMW's R100RS sports-tourer cost £2900 and Yamaha's new XS750 just £1400). Just seven had been built by 1980, when production was taken over by Romarsh of Calne in Wiltshire; and that firm produced only ten more before going bust two years later. Newell updated the concept to produce the much more rapid Phasar, powered by Kawasaki's six-cylinder Z1300 engine, but only a few were built.

SPECIFICATIONS	QUASAR (1976)
Engine	Liquid-cooled ohv eight-valve four
Capacity	848cc (82.5 x 89.9mm)
Maximum power	40bhp @ 5500rpm
Transmission	Four-speed, shaft final drive
Frame	Steel space-frame
Suspension	Pivoted front fork; twin shock rear
Brakes	Disc front and rear
Weight	690lb (313kg)
Top speed	100mph (161km/h)

Raleigh

Bicycles have always been Raleigh's main game, but the firm from Nottingham has also dabbled in the production of motorbikes from time to time. Its first venture was short-lived. Raleigh was among Britain's motorcycling pioneers, and in 1899 produced a machine powered by a Schwann engine placed above the front wheel. Four years later the firm was building 3hp bikes featuring a clutch and twistgrip throttle, but production stopped in 1905.

*R*ALEIGH'S SECOND and most productive motorcycling spell began in 1921 with the Model 9, an innovative longitudinal flat-twin of 699cc capacity. The side-valve motor was fitted with a three-speed gearbox made by Sturmey-Archer, a Raleigh subsidiary. Unusually, it featured rear springing, with a swingarm that pivoted on the gearbox casing. Other features included Brampton Bi-flex girder forks, quickly detachable wheels and a front brake that acted on a dummy wheel rim.

The Model 9 was intended for solo or sidecar use. But performance was unimpressive even when ridden solo, with a top

SPECIFICATIONS	RALEIGH MODEL 9 (1921)
Engine	Air-cooled side-valve four-valve flat-twin
Capacity	699cc (77 x 75mm)
Maximum power	Not known
Transmission	Three-speed, chain final drive
Frame	Steel twin cradle
Suspension	Girder front; leaf-spring rear
Brakes	Dummy rim front; drum rear
Weight	290lb (132kg)
Top speed	52mph (84km/h)

speed of only just over 50mph (80km/h), and the bike was expensive to produce. From 1924 it was replaced by a 799cc V-twin, and during the 1920s Raleigh also built a varied string of other models, including a tiny 174cc side-valve single.

Sensing that its name lacked the real class to attract enthusiasts, Raleigh embarked on a racing programme to change its image. 'Wizard' O'Donovan, the legendary Norton tuner, was hired to direct operations and built some special racing bikes, but the firm's best result at the TT was fifth in the Junior in 1930.

In 1931 Raleigh introduced a new single-cylinder model that followed the trend towards 'sloper' cylinder layout. But sales were poor and Raleigh again abandoned motorcycle production. In 1958 the firm made another return by making mopeds, then it built Mobylette and Bianchi machines from Italy under licence, notably a 78cc Bianchi scooter that was sold as the Raleigh Roma in the UK. But that venture ended in 1967, and from this time on there has been no comeback.

Above and left: Raleigh's 799cc V-twin of 1924 produced 7hp – enough to pull a loaded sidecar, albeit not at any great speed.

Rex

Rex was one of the sportiest marques of motorcycling's early years, earning a fine reputation for racing success and record-breaking long-distance runs. Star rider Wal Handley won grands prix and TTs for the Coventry firm, whose badge in later years incorporated the Isle of Man's three-legged symbol.

Below left: Rex-Acme's name was closely associated with competition success.

Below right: This 350cc single dates from 1925, the year of Wal Hanley's TT double.

*R*EX MOTORCYCLES came into being in 1900 when brothers Billy and Harold Williamson built a 1.75hp single. By 1906 Rex had become well established, with a 465cc side–valve single and a 726cc V-twin, and had produced an early version of telescopic front forks with an exposed spring between twin stanchions on each leg. A year later Billy Heaton used the system when taking third place in the twin-cylinder class at the first Isle of Man TT.

The Williamsons left Rex in 1911 (Billy later produced a 1000cc flat-twin under his own name) but the firm's success continued under new boss George Hemmingway. Rex used JAP engines for a separate range of Rex-JAP bikes, produced for the Premier firm, and built complete machines for sale under its own name. In 1921 the firm became Rex-Acme, after taking over the Coventry Acme Motor Company next door. Engine production was abandoned and the firm's large range of bikes used Blackburne, JAP and other powerplants ranging from 170cc to 750cc.

SPECIFICATIONS	REX-ACME 350 (1926)
Engine	Air-cooled ohv four-valve single
Capacity	348cc (71 x 88mm)
Maximum power	30bhp approx
Transmission	Three-speed, chain final drive
Frame	Steel diamond
Suspension	Girder front; rigid rear
Brakes	Drum front and rear
Weight	223lb (101kg)
Top speed	65mph (105km/h)

Handley's racing success in the 1920s included the first-ever TT double in 1925, with wins in the Lightweight and Junior events. He finished second on a 500cc V-twin in the Senior a year later, and won the Lightweight again in 1927, adding victory in that year's 200-mile (322km) sidecar race at Brooklands. But these and other victories were not enough to keep Rex-Acme alive through the Depression. Production was briefly revived by the Mills–Fulford sidecar firm, but ended for good in 1933.

Rickman

Brothers Don and Derek Rickman were motocross stars who set up in business in Hampshire in the late 1950s. They began by building motocross bikes (scramblers, as they were then known) combining Triumph engines with BSA frames, using the name Métisse, French for mongrel. The Rickmans also built their own high-quality chassis, using frames made from Reynolds 531 tubing.

Below left: Rickman's Interceptor was arguably too good for its ageing Enfield Constellation engine.

Below right: The Rickman brothers began by building scramblers such as this 1962-model Métisse Mk I.

*R*ICKMAN ALSO earned a good reputation for roadster and racing chassis, and in 1970 produced an outstanding all-British bike in the Rickman Interceptor. This was the result of Royal Enfield going out of business, leaving a large batch of 750cc twin-cylinder Constellation engines with no frames. Enfield's US export agent commissioned Rickman to build a series of bikes to make use of them.

The resultant sports machine combined high bars, fibreglass tank and seat, Rickman duplex-cradle frame and top-class cycle parts. The Rickman Interceptor looked good, handled superbly and was much lighter than the Constellation, although Rickman could do nothing about the 56bhp twin's vibration and poor gearbox. A total of 137 Rickman Interceptors were built.

Rickman continued to build a variety of bikes, many of them off-road machines, and in the early 1970s produced over 10,000 two-strokes with 125cc and 250cc engines. The majority of Rickman's bikes were sold abroad, earning a Queen's Award for exports. The Hampshire firm also created some stylish and fine-handling roadgoing superbikes based on Japanese engines, notably Honda's four-cylinder CB750 and Kawasaki's Z1000.

These café-racers featured fairings and tank/seat units made from fibreglass, another Rickman speciality. The firm produced huge numbers of fairings, panniers and top-boxes, which were sold both under the Rickman name and also as Hondastyle accessories. Metal accessories such as engine protection bars and luggage racks were other profitable Rickman lines in the 1980s.

SPECIFICATIONS	RICKMAN INTERCEPTOR (1970)
Engine	Air-cooled ohv four-valve parallel twin
Capacity	736cc (71 x 93mm)
Maximum power	56bhp @ 6750rpm
Transmission	Four-speed, chain final drive
Frame	Steel twin cradle
Suspension	Telescopic front; twin shocks rear
Brakes	Disc front and rear
Weight	353lb (160kg)
Top speed	110mph (177km/h)

Royal Enfield Bullet

After starting life as a bicycle manufacturer in the late Victorian era, like so many of its rivals, Royal Enfield soon carved out a distinct identity. Over the years the firm from Redditch, south of Birmingham, became known first for V-twins, then for singles including the Bullet models, and also for parallel twins of particularly large capacity.

*D*ESPITE THE 'Royal' title (derived from the Enfield Cycle Company's links with the Royal Small Arms factory in Enfield, Middlesex), Enfield never quite matched the glamour or popularity of rivals such as Triumph and Norton. One early model that did prove its speed was the 3hp V-twin that came close to winning the Isle of Man TT in 1914. The V-twin had been introduced the year before with a capacity of 425cc, and was reduced to 350cc to comply with racing regulations.

The inlet-over-exhaust V-twin's outstanding technical feature was an automatic dry-sump lubrication system, which gave it a big advantage at a time when other machines relied on the rider

remembering to use a hand-operated oil pump. Enfield rider F.J. Walker took third place at the TT but was killed when he crashed into a barrier after crossing the finishing line.

In this period Enfield was also known for another V-twin machine, the 6hp, 770cc JAP-engined Model No 180, which typically pulled a fully upholstered 'torpedo'-shaped wicker sidecar. That engine was uprated to 8hp after the First World War, when Major Frank Smith, one of three sons of the firm's founder Robert Smith, returned to occupy the position of assistant managing director. Major Smith took over Enfield in 1933, and would head the firm until his death in 1962.

Opposite top and below: In its early years Royal Enfield was best known for its V-twins, which were popular for both solo and sidecar use. This bike features the swept-back handlebars and girder front suspension that were common features at the time, and also has front and rear brakes working on dummy wheel rims.

Right: Royal Enfield introduced the uprated 350cc Bullet single in 1949, complete with alloy head and swingarm rear suspension. Fifty years later, 500cc versions such as this are still being built in India and exported to Britain and elsewhere, with remarkably few modifications.

In the late 1920s and early 1930s Enfield produced a 976cc side-valve V-twin that was well suited to pulling a sidecar, and the firm continued in similar vein with the Model K of 1939. This was also a side-valve V-twin, its 1140cc capacity being exceeded only by the exotic Brough Superior. Sidecar gearing came as standard, because the Model K was essentially designed to be a workhorse. Its chair was used for everything from transporting builder's cement to selling ice-cream.

But it was for lighter and simpler singles that the Redditch firm became better known. In 1924 the firm had entered the 350cc single market with a sporty overhead-valve JAP-engined model, and also produced a 350cc side-valve engine of its own. The famous

Bullet name was introduced in the early 1930s, following Enfield's introduction in 1930 of a line of 500cc, 350cc and (from 1933) 250cc singles.

The most interesting of the early Bullets was the 500cc JFL31, which featured a four-valve cylinder head. The factory claimed this gave an extra 3hp, and with higher compression made the Bullet good for 85mph (137km/h). Enfield said that with taller gearing and a little more preparation the 500 was good for a 'ton'. To prove it, the Bullet was independently tested over a flying quarter-mile. Its 99mph (159km/h) average speed was regarded by most as close enough to the magic mark.

In 1949 Enfield introduced an all-new 350 Bullet. This combined swingarm suspension with an all-new engine featuring an alloy cylinder head, redesigned camshaft assembly and more compact crankcase design. A 500cc version followed in 1952. The Bullet made a lively, fine-handling and reliable roadster and was also used successfully in trials.

Enfield's sportier singles of the 1960s included the Crusader and the racy Continental GT. But it was the humble Bullet that would far outlast them all. Bullet production had begun under licence in Madras, India, in the 1950s. And although UK production ceased in 1963, the Bullet is still built in Madras, in only slightly updated form, to this day.

SPECIFICATIONS	ROYAL ENFIELD 350 BULLET (1949)
Engine	Air-cooled ohv two-valve single
Capacity	346cc (70 x 90mm)
Maximum power	18bhp @ 5750rpm
Transmission	Four-speed, chain final drive
Frame	Steel single downtube
Suspension	Telescopic front; twin shocks rear
Brakes	Drum front and rear
Weight	350lb (159kg)
Top speed	75mph (121km/h)

Royal Enfield Constellation

There was something distinctive about the big twin-cylinder roadsters that Royal Enfield produced in the 1950s and '60s. Their unusual capacity and styling helped them to stand apart from the ranks of more traditional British parallel twins.

All pictures: The Constellation's unusually large capacity gave good performance, but the parallel twin lacked reliability.

*T*HE REDDITCH firm did produce a parallel twin of conventional 500cc capacity in 1949, but replaced it in 1953 with the Meteor, whose capacity of 692cc came about because its engine was produced by combining two 346cc single-cylinder Bullet engines. (Further economy was achieved by using the crankcases from the 500cc bike.) The first Meteor's softly tuned engine produced only a modest 36bhp, but this was raised to 40bhp in 1956 with the release of the Super Meteor.

Two years later, the Constellation arrived with a comprehensively revamped powerplant. The list of modifications included hotter camshafts positioned higher in the engine, lighter pushrods, reworked valves and cylinder heads, a stronger crankshaft, higher 8.5:1 compression ratio, extra cylinder finning for better

cooling, a new clutch and lower gearing. Claimed power output was up to 51bhp at 6250rpm.

In characteristic Enfield tradition the motor formed a stressed member of the frame, which was similar to that of the Super Meteor, with a single downtube and no tubes underneath. Most cycle parts were also borrowed from the Super Meteor, but the Constellation stood out thanks to its chrome-and-maroon tank, siamesed exhaust system and the 150mph Smith's speedometer in its headlamp nacelle.

The original Constellation was a rapid machine. During tests one bike was clocked at 116mph (187km/h), giving it an edge over rival twins, and an early press test recorded an equally impressive two-way average top speed of 112mph (180km/h). Very few bikes

Enfield's Racing Exploits

Competition success might have been the spark that would make Constellation sales take off, but Enfield's efforts didn't have the desired effect. The factory tried hard, particularly in the prestigious Thruxton 500-mile production race, in which the Redditch firm's team was run by top tuner Syd Lawton. Enfield's star rider Bob McIntyre led the race four years in a row but always hit problems.

McIntyre and Enfield came a respectable third in 1958, behind Triumph-mounted Mike Hailwood. But a year later the hard-riding Scot crashed out of the race as he tried to make up ground after a clutch problem. Worse was to come, as in each of the next two years' events he was thrown off at high speed on account of engine failure. Sadly for Royal Enfield, those Thruxton disappointments seemed to sum up the fast but flawed Constellation all too accurately.

SPECIFICATIONS	ROYAL ENFIELD CONSTELLATION (1963)
Engine	Air-cooled ohv four-valve flat-twin
Capacity	692cc (70 x 90mm)
Maximum power	51bhp @ 6250rpm
Transmission	Four-speed, chain final drive
Frame	Steel single downtube
Suspension	Telescopic front; twin shocks rear
Brakes	Drum front and rear
Weight	403lb (183kg)
Top speed	112mph (180km/h)

on the road could live with the Constellation over the standing quarter mile, and the big motor had plenty of low-down torque too, which made it an easy bike to ride fast.

But Royal Enfield's hopes that the Constellation's straight-line speed would result in big sales were soon dashed, largely because when ridden hard the big twin developed problems including oil leaks, blowing head gaskets and conrod failure at high revs. During its five-year existence the Constellation gained low 'ace' handlebars, plus numerous engine updates, including revised crankcase breathing, in an attempt to silence the 'Royal Oilfield' comments.

In 1962 Royal Enfield introduced the 750cc Interceptor, becoming the first British manufacturer to respond to the American market's demands for a larger-capacity parallel twin. The Interceptor was fast and torquey, and its dynamically balanced crankshaft helped make for a reasonably smooth ride. But neither that bike nor the redesigned Interceptor Mk II of 1968 could save Royal Enfield, which had been taken over by Norton Villiers.

The Interceptor survived the closure of the Redditch factory, as the final machines were built at Enfield's underground engine plant near Bradford-on-Avon in Wiltshire. But production finally ended in 1970, when the last batch of engines was used to power the Rickman Interceptor sportster.

Rudge

Rudge-Whitworth was formed when Whitworth Cycles acquired Rudge, another Midlands bicycle firm, in 1894. Motorcycle production began in 1911, with a 500cc single. Rudge rider Victor Surridge proved its ability by lapping Brooklands at 66.47mph (106.95km/h), a record at that time for a 500cc bike.

Below left: This 245cc Rudge Rapid dates from 1937, shortly after the firm's period of greatest racing success.

Below right: Rudge used four-valve heads to good effect in the years around 1926, when this 500cc bike was built.

E ARLY INNOVATIONS included a spring-up stand and a hinged rear mudguard (to aid wheel removal), but it was a system of gearing that led to the firm's first famous model: the Rudge Multi. This used a pulley arrangement to maintain the tension of the final drive belt, allowing the rider to select from no fewer than 21 gear ratios using a long lever. The Multi was launched on the market in 1912 at a cost of £5 more than the standard single-gear model, and remained in production until 1923.

Rudge earned a great reputation for racing after a tragic start. In the Isle of Man in 1911, the first year the TT was held over the full Mountain circuit, Surridge crashed at Glen Helen and became the first rider to be killed in a TT. Two years later disaster struck again when Frank Bateman, leading on a Rudge, crashed and was killed. Rudge might still have won the race, but Ray Abbott entered the last bend with his Multi in high gear rather than low, stalled his engine, and lost by five seconds. But Cyril Pullin scored a first success for Rudge in 1914, winning the Senior TT at an average of almost 50mph (80km/h).

Rudge had been working on a V-twin design, but the First World War intervened and the 998cc machine could not be introduced until 1919. This too was available with the Multi gear, known then as the Multwin. But by this time the belt drive

arrangement had become outdated. Rudge finally introduced a three-speed gearbox in 1920, and a chain-drive model, powered by a 499cc single engine the following year.

The firm was a leading exponent of four-valve cylinder heads in the mid-1920s, producing the 500cc single on which Graham Walker (the firm's sales manager; later a journalist and the father of television commentator Murray) won the 1928 Ulster Grand Prix. The sportiest of Rudge's three models was renamed the Ulster in recognition, and the name was used on the firm's high-performance models for the next decade.

The Ulster used the firm's celebrated linked braking system, whereby the foot-pedal operated both front and rear drums, with the hand-lever also working the front brake. The single's performance was impressive, with a top speed of over 90mph (145km/h) that led to the bike being advertised as 'probably the fastest 500cc motorcycle in normal production'.

Rudge had more racing success in the 1930s, under the guidance of race team boss George Hack. The marque won the Junior and Senior TT double in 1931, and in the following year Rudge's brand new four-valve 250 finished first, second and fourth at the TT. Three years later it went even better by securing the first three places as Jimmy Simpson took his only TT win.

In normal times such racing success would have been reflected in the showrooms, but it was Rudge's misfortune that the firm's best period coincided with the worst recession the motorcycle trade had ever seen. The high costs of racing had hit the company, too. Rudge turned to selling engines under the Python label, but in 1933 the receiver was called in and the racing department closed.

The firm's boss John Pugh died three years later. New owners Gramophone Ltd (who made radio equipment and records as HMV and, later, EMI) moved Rudge to Middlesex. But when the Second World War started in 1939 the factory was requisitioned to make electronic equipment, bringing bike production to an end.

Above: Rudge used the Ulster name until production ended in 1939, the year this 500cc bike was built.

Below: The Multi's pulley arrangement provides no fewer than 21 gear ratios, selected using a long lever.

SPECIFICATIONS	RUDGE ULSTER (1933)
Engine	Air-cooled ohv four-valve single
Capacity	499cc (85 x 88mm)
Maximum power	30bhp @ 5200rpm
Transmission	Four-speed, chain final drive
Frame	Steel twin downtube
Suspension	Girder front; rigid rear
Brakes	Drum front and rear
Weight	298lb (135kg)
Top speed	93mph (150km/h)

Scott

Alfred Angas Scott was one of early motorcycling's most inspirational figures. As well as creating the two-stroke parallel twins for which he is best remembered, the Yorkshireman was responsible for a long list of technical innovations, including kick-starters, rotary induction valves, triangulated frames, unit-construction engines, and the caliper brake for which, in 1897, he was granted the first of more than 50 patents.

*S*COTT'S FIRST engine was a two-stroke parallel twin unit that he fixed to a bicycle. In 1904 he began production of a motorcycle combining a development of this with his triangulated frame. His first six bikes, powered by a water-cooled 333cc two-stroke twin unit, were built at the Bradford premises of the Jowett brothers. When they decided to concentrate on car production, Scott set up on his own nearby.

Apart from their unusual engine design, the Scott Engineering Company's early models were notable for such novelties as a kickstart, foot-change two-speed gearbox and telescopic front forks. Capacity grew to from 450cc to 486cc, cooled by an uprated system incorporating a patented honeycomb radiator.

The simple and light two-stroke twins provided excellent performance, and Scotts began earning a strong competition reputation. Numerous wins in hillclimbs and trials events were capped in 1912 when Frank Applebee won the Senior TT at an average speed of over 48mph (77km/h), becoming the first two-stroke rider to do so and also the first to lead from start to finish. Orders came flooding in, and Scott moved to a new factory in nearby Shipley.

Scott rider Tim Wood repeated the Senior TT victory in 1913, but the First World War broke out a year later and the factory became involved in production of a gun-carrying sidecar outfit and a three-wheeled car. When the War ended, Alfred Scott sold his

Opposite: This 1929-model Squirrel was one of the last with Scott's early barrel fuel tank layout.

Above: By 1949 the 596cc Flying Squirrel was more conventional, but also less competitive.

interest in the bike firm to concentrate on producing a civilian version of the three-wheeler, the Scott Sociable, also powered by a two-stroke twin. The Sociable sold poorly, especially after the arrival of the popular Austin Seven car. In 1922 Scott died of pneumonia at the age of 48.

The Scott Engineering Co continued to produce bikes along familiar lines, and in the early 1920s introduced the Squirrel, a sporting 486cc version of the existing 532cc model. In 1924 this led

SPECIFICATIONS	SCOTT FLYING SQUIRREL (1925)
Engine	Water-cooled two-stroke parallel twin
Capacity	596cc (74.6 x 68.25mm)
Maximum power	25bhp @ 5000rpm
Transmission	Three-speed, chain final drive
Frame	Triangulated tubular steel
Suspension	Telescopic front; rigid rear
Brakes	Drum front and rear
Weight	253lb (115kg)
Top speed	70mph (113km/h)

to the Super Squirrel, whose new 498cc or 596cc engine featured a liquid-cooled cylinder head as well as barrel. The first three-speed model, the Flying Squirrel, was launched two years later.

By this time Scotts had begun to struggle against increasingly powerful four-strokes in racing, but the firm's third place in the 1928 Senior TT resulted in a Flying Squirrel-based TT Replica model for the following year. By now the early layout of open frame and barrel fuel tank beneath the saddle had been replaced by a full-frame design with a more conventionally placed tank.

The Yorkshire firm's growing problems culminated in 1931 with the official receiver being called in. An enthusiast named Albert Reynolds attempted a rescue, but without lasting success. Plans for a new 650cc twin were dropped. And although Scott generated a flurry of interest at the Olympia Show in 1934 by unveiling the prototype Model 3S, a two-stroke triple with 747cc (and later 986cc) capacity, this too failed to reach volume production.

After the Second World War Scott briefly resumed production of the 596cc rigid-framed Flying Squirrel, updated from girder to telescopic forks. But the bikes were heavy, underpowered and expensive, and few were sold. In 1950 the firm was bought by Birmingham-based Scott enthusiast Matt Holder. He added a swing-arm frame and continued developing and selling Squirrels in tiny numbers right up until 1978.

Seeley

Colin Seeley followed a successful career as a sidecar racer – he won the British championship in 1962 and '63 – by producing a string of fine-handling motorcycles powered by a wide variety of engines.

Below: Seeley G50s won many races in the late 1960s and early 1970s, and in recent years bikes such as this one, being ridden by Chris McGahan, have been hugely successful in classic racing.

*T*HOSE CHAMPIONSHIPS were won with Matchless-engined outfits. Seeley, who was also a Matchless dealer, began by acquiring manufacturing rights to the G50 and AJS 7R racers in 1966, following the closure of the AMC race shop.

Realizing the limitations of the racers' original chassis, Seeley designed and built a much stiffer and lighter frame, using Reynolds 531 tubing, that gave the single-cylinder engine a new lease of life. The Seeley G50 was raced to many wins by riders including Derek Minter, John Blanchard and John Cooper, and in recent years it has also been very successful in classic racing.

By the start of the 1970s, Seeley's 27-strong firm, based at Belvedere in Kent, was established as one of the world's leading chassis and racebike constructors. The Seeley G50 racer was modified to produce a sporty single-cylinder roadster, the Condor, an exotic machine of which only seven were ever built. Other all-British projects included a Weslake-engined 750cc parallel twin and the Kuhn-Seeley, which combined Norton's twin-cylinder Commando engine with an updated Mk III Seeley frame.

Some of the Kent firm's most successful bikes used foreign engines. Seeley designed the frames used by Ducati's legendary V-twin racebikes of the early 1970s, and his drive-chain adjustment system was used on the Italian firm's road bikes. At Barry Sheene's suggestion, Seeley produced a chassis for Suzuki's evil-handling 500cc two-stroke twin in 1971. And after Seeley had developed a bike based on Honda's four-cylinder CB750 engine, Honda UK commissioned the firm to build a batch of official limited-edition superbikes using the same motor.

SPECIFICATIONS	SEELEY G50 (1966)
Engine	Air-cooled ohc two-valve single
Capacity	499cc (90 x 87mm)
Maximum power	51bhp @ 7100rpm
Transmission	Five-speed, chain final drive
Frame	Steel twin cradle
Suspension	Telescopic front; twin shocks rear
Brakes	Twin drum front; drum rear
Weight	295lb (134kg)
Top speed	133mph (214km/h)

Silk

George Silk was a great Scott enthusiast, and the 700S that he built in the 1970s was in many ways a logical development of the famous Yorkshire marque's two-stroke parallel twins. While working as an apprentice for Derbyshire-based Scott specialist Tom Ward, George began modifying the two-strokes for vintage racing. Eventually he founded Silk Engineering, in partnership with Maurice Patey, to produce the 700S.

Below left and right: The Silk was a handsome bike, and its combination of light weight, rigid frame and excellent suspension gave fine handling by 1970s superbike standards.

ILK'S 653cc engine strongly resembled its Scott predecessors, but differed in key areas including its use of electronic ignition, a new wet multiplate clutch plus conventional bearings and lubrication system. The engine was very light and compact and, although it produced only 47bhp at 6000rpm, it had a broad power spread and produced maximum torque at just 3000rpm. Performance was undramatic, but the bike was good for 110mph (177km/h) and fairly smooth.

Chassis design was very different from that of the old Scotts, as the Silk had a modern tubular-steel frame made by Spondon Engineering. The 700S was very small and light, weighing just 310lb (141kg). Its rigid frame, high-quality Spondon forks and firm Girling shocks gave superb handling. Less impressive were the poor low-speed running (partly due to the four-speed gearbox's tall first ratio), difficult kickstart and lack of electric starter.

The 700S was expensive and production levels were low, partly due to the difficulty of obtaining electrical and other components in the small numbers required. In 1976 Silk was taken over by the

Furmanite International group, its largest stockholder. Production continued, and in 1978 the 100th bike was built, by now in Mk II form with power increased to 54bhp, left-foot gearchange and twin discs as standard. But despite a further price rise, the Silk was not profitable, and the last one left the factory in December 1979.

SPECIFICATIONS	SILK 700S (1976)
Engine	Liquid-cooled two-stroke parallel twin
Capacity	653cc (76 x 72mm)
Maximum power	47bhp @ 7000rpm
Transmission	Four-speed, chain final drive
Frame	Steel twin cradle
Suspension	Telescopic front; twin shocks rear
Brakes	Disc front and rear
Weight	310lb (141kg)
Top speed	110mph (177km/h)

Sunbeam Model 9

High quality roadsters and a string of racing victories made Sunbeam one of the most respected and popular marques in the first part of the 20th century. Sunbeam was also notable for the age of its founder. John Marston was no less than 76 years old, and had been in business for over 50 years, when he built his first motorcycle in 1912.

THE MARSTON family had been pioneers in japanning, the process by which metal is given a high-gloss baked finish. The Sunbeam name was used for products ranging from enamelware and kitchen utensils to luxury bicycles and a prototype car. The bicycles built at the large Wolverhampton factory known as Sunbeamland were marketed as 'The Gentleman's Bicycle' (there was also a Ladies' version), and the first powered machine had a similar high-quality character.

Like the firm's bicycles, it featured a fully-enclosed drive chain that earned it the nickname 'Little Oil Bath'. The 350cc single was designed by John Greenwood, who was highly regarded for his work at Rover motorcycles. Its other advanced features included a two-speed gearbox, multi-plate clutch and an ingenious divided-axle system on the rear wheel, which enabled a punctured inner tube to be removed for repair without disturbing the wheel or chain.

That first model was quickly followed by a 770cc JAP-powered V-twin that used a new three-speed gearbox of Sunbeam's own design. The gearbox was also used on the firm's first 500cc single, which followed shortly afterwards. This bike was used for Sunbeam's first attempt at the TT, in 1914. A three-man team including Howard Davies, later to found HRD, performed strongly and was awarded the Manufacturer's Team prize, although the race organizers later changed their minds after a recount.

John Marston died in 1918, followed shortly afterwards by his son Roland, and the family was forced to sell the business to pay large death duties. But Sunbeam's motorcycle production continued to thrive under its new owners, Noble Industries (later to become chemical giant ICI). Indeed the 1920s was to be the firm's most glorious period, with a string of competition successes from star riders including Tommy de la Hay, George Dance and Charlie Dodson.

Dance was more of a sprint and hillclimb ace than a road-racer, but he set the fastest lap in the 1920 Senior TT, which was won by teammate de la Hay. Two years later Sunbeam struck again when Alec Bennett, also riding the 500cc side-valve single, known as the

Right: The Model 9 of the 1930s was powered by a 493cc single motor and finished in Sunbeam's traditional black and gold. This bike was built in 1939 at Plumstead, following Sunbeam's takeover by Matchless.

Below: The earlier Model 8 combines a similar pushrod single engine with hand gearchange.

'Longstroke' due to its 77 x 105mm cylinder dimensions, set new race and lap records on his way to Senior victory.

In 1923 Sunbeam added an overhead-valve single, in both 500cc and 350cc capacities. Dance broke down in that year's Junior TT while leading, but later set 350cc world speed records and was almost unbeatable in sprints and hillclimbs. Graham Walker joined Sunbeam in 1924 as rider and competitions manager, and scored some impressive victories. But Walker was a Rudge-mounted rival

SPECIFICATIONS	SUNBEAM MODEL 9 (1937)
Engine	Air-cooled ohv two-valve single
Capacity	493cc (80 x 98mm)
Maximum power	25bhp @ 6000rpm
Transmission	Four-speed, chain final drive
Frame	Steel single downtube
Suspension	Girder front; rigid rear
Brakes	Drum front and rear
Weight	320lb (145kg) approx
Top speed	75mph (121km/h)

at the TT in 1928, when Charlie Dodson beat him to win for Sunbeam. Dodson won the Senior again a year later, as Sunbeam took the team award for the third successive year.

Sunbeam's roadster development had been somewhat overlooked during the years of competition success, and during the Depression of the 1930s the range was cut to four models. Three were overhead-valve machines: the 493cc Model 9 tourer and sportier Model 90, plus a new and inexpensive 344cc single. The old 'Longstroke' side-valver lived on in the Lion model.

The firm's fortunes appeared to be rising, but in 1936 Sunbeam was bought by Matchless, which had acquired AJS four years earlier. The three marques were combined to form Associated Motor Cycles (AMC), and Sunbeam motorcycle production was transferred to the Matchless base at Plumstead, south London.

Sunbeam S7

The second half of the Sunbeam saga began when the company was bought by BSA in 1943, during the Second World War. The giant Birmingham firm, which had already received from the British government some captured examples of BMW's R75 flat-twin sidecar outfit, was keen to develop a flagship model. Sunbeam's upmarket image, so BSA's thinking went, would be ideally suited to a high-quality machine based on the BMW.

Below: With its huge balloon tyres and distinctive green paintwork the S7 was a striking and rather handsome machine, but the 500cc tandem twin's engine performance, handling, braking and reliability all failed to justify the high price.

A FLAT-TWIN layout similar to the BMW was regarded as too obvious and likely to encounter anti-German feeling. Designer Erling Poppe, whose background included work with buses and lorries as well as bikes, instead produced a 487cc overhead-cam tandem twin unit, which incorporated many BMW details including shaft drive and a rear-mounted gearbox.

The S7, launched in 1947 and produced at BSA's factory in Redditch, south of Birmingham, was an undeniably striking machine. It featured mist-green paint, balloon tyres and large skirted mudguards, and had a distinct air of luxury. It was advertised as 'the world's most magnificent motor cycle', and at £222 was certainly one of the most expensive.

But the S7 suffered from a number of basic design flaws and was also a serious disappointment on the road. For a 500cc twin it was slow, with a top speed of 75mph (121km/h), and too heavy at 435lb (197kg). It handled poorly thanks partly to its huge tyres, and it had feeble brakes. Its 25bhp motor was not particularly economical, a much more important consideration in those days than now, and also it developed a reputation for unreliability, with recurring problems including overheating, cracked cylinder liners and main bearing failure.

Nor was the S7 helped by BSA's attempts to promote it. Some early bikes were sent to South Africa to be ridden by the local police force during a visit by King George VI – and were returned

Left and below: The S8's traditional Sunbeam black finish and normal-sized tyres made it a more conventional machine than the S7. Engine changes added power and reliability, making a competent and much more practical motorbike, and the S8's rubber-mounted engine gave a notably smooth ride. Handling was improved by chassis changes including the adoption of front forks from parent company BSA.

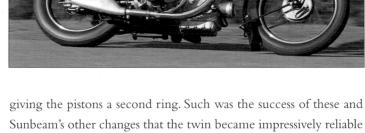

because they vibrated so badly that they were unridable. And when Sunbeam later tried to present an S7 to Second World War hero Field Marshal Montgomery at the London Motor Cycle Show, the firm's stand collapsed.

Given all these drawbacks, it was hardly surprising that only 2000 bikes had been built by Spring 1949, two years later. This was when Sunbeam tried to fight back with the new and sportier S8. This kept the S7's format of a 487cc air-cooled in-line parallel twin engine with shaft final drive. But the S8 was finished in Sunbeam's traditional black, and replaced the S7's fat 16-inch tyres with narrower conventional rubber. (The S7 De Luxe, introduced at the same time, retained the original model's styling.)

The new powerplant was slightly more powerful, thanks to increased compression and a new exhaust system, but most of its changes were aimed at improving reliability. Extra oil capacity dramatically reduced the overheating problem. The S7's high oil consumption, a cause of its main bearing failures, was reduced by

giving the pistons a second ring. Such was the success of these and Sunbeam's other changes that the twin became impressively reliable and its reputation was restored.

BSA retained the S7's twin-downtube steel frame but gave the S8 a major handling improvement with new front forks, as well as narrower wheels and tyres. Its forks were conventional telescopics, in place of the S7's unsuccessful design, which had a single spring between the legs and no hydraulic damping. Rear suspension was by plunger, as before, backed up by a sprung single saddle.

The S8 was slightly faster than its predecessor and handled better. It was considerably more popular, and more than 10,000 had been sold by the end of 1952. But it was not good enough. Development stagnated, demand fell, and in 1957 BSA halted production of not just the S8, but of all Sunbeam motorcycles. Apart from one final insult when BSA used the famous name on a couple of scooters, another of the great old British marques was dead.

SPECIFICATIONS	SUNBEAM S7 (1947)
Engine	Air-cooled ohc four-valve tandem twin
Capacity	487cc (70x 63.5mm)
Maximum power	25bhp @ 5800rpm
Transmission	Four-speed, shaft final drive
Frame	Steel single downtube
Suspension	Telescopic front; plunger rear
Brakes	Drum front and rear
Weight	435lb (197kg)
Top speed	75mph (121km/h)

Triton

The name Triton does not refer to one particular firm, as this classic combination of Triumph parallel twin engine and Norton frame was created by a variety of companies and individuals. But in its 1960s heyday, the Triton, much more so than similar hybrids such as Tribsa and Norvin, became established as a marque in its own right.

Below: The combination of a 650cc Triumph Bonneville motor in a Manx Norton Featherbed frame was just about the ultimate in performance in the 1960s.

A TRITON WAS the ultimate café racer, and also proved its class on the racetrack with wins in many prestigious production and endurance events.

Nobody knows for sure who built the first Triton, and it's likely that several individuals did so independently of one another in the mid-1950s. One early constructor was a London racer/engineer called Doug Clark, who fitted a Triumph 650cc engine into a frame from a blown-up Manx Norton in 1954. The bike was used both on road and track, as Clark rode his hybrid machine to the circuits where he was competing.

Triumph was reportedly less than pleased at the development. An official from the Meriden factory noticed the Triton when it was raced for the first time at Silverstone. Shortly afterwards, owner Clark later revealed, he received a letter from Triumph, threatening legal action if he continued with the project. The firm even told its London dealers to refuse to sell him engine spares.

Triumph's hostility could not prevent the Triton's steady increase in popularity, which was accelerated in the early 1960s when firms including Dresda Autos of west London began producing conversion kits and complete machines. Dresda boss

Paul Dunstall – King of the Café Racers

If the Triton was the finest café racer of the 1960s, and the Dresda Triton its best known exponent, it was Paul Dunstall who did most to establish the cult of the racy British twin. Dunstall began by tuning his own roadgoing Norton Dominator, then took to the racetrack where his fast and immaculately prepared machinery brought rapid success. Before long he had given up selling scooters to produce go-faster parts, especially for the Norton, including clip-ons, rearsets, petrol tanks, fairings, high-compression pistons and cylinder heads.

By 1967 Dunstall was producing complete Dunstall Norton machines, and his firm was registered as a manufacturer by the taxation authorities. His most successful product was the famous Decibel silencer, of which over 30,000 per year were sold at one stage. Dunstall Triumphs followed, as did Dunstall Suzukis following the Japanese rise to motorcycling dominance in the 1970s. When demand dropped in the 1980s, Dunstall sold out to concentrate on property development.

Below left: A trio of Tritons shows, from left, 650cc Wideline Featherbed, 650cc Manx and 750cc Dresda variations on the theme. Tritons were – and still are – essentially hand-built to the owner's specification.

Below right: Whether you were racing officially at Brands Hatch or simply scratching from one roadside café to the next, Norton's Featherbed-based chassis gave peerless handling.

Dave Degens was a leading racer, and his victory (with co-rider Rex Butcher) on a Triton in the 24-hour race at Montjuic Park in Barcelona in 1965 led to a big increase in demand.

Degens, who won the same race again on a similar machine five years later, estimates that his firm built over 500 Tritons in the 1960s and early 1970s, plus many Featherbed-style frames around which owners assembled Tritons of their own. Detail differences

SPECIFICATIONS	DRESDA TRITON (1965)
Engine	Air-cooled ohv four-valve Triumph parallel twin
Capacity	649cc (71 x 82mm)
Maximum power	50bhp @ 6500rpm
Transmission	Four-speed, chain final drive
Frame	Steel duplex cradle Norton Featherbed
Suspension	Telescopic front; twin shocks rear
Brakes	Drum front and rear
Weight	350lb (159kg)
Top speed	120mph (193km/h)

abounded, as no two Tritons were ever identical. Bikes were built with a wide variety of petrol tanks, seats, suspension parts, exhaust systems and even fairings.

Engines ranged from 500cc pre-unit devices to later 750cc unit-construction twins, with the twin-carburettor 650cc Triumph Bonneville motor being most popular. The choice of frame included Slimline and the earlier Wideline Featherbeds, plus original Manx Norton frames, as well as reproductions from Dresda and other chassis specialists.

Although it was essentially a mongrel, the Triton's style, racing record and café racer reputation gave it a lasting charisma that few pure-bred bikes approached. Dresda moved on to produce chassis for Japanese bikes in the 1970s. But the Triton has become more popular again in recent years, and small numbers are still built at Dresda's workshop near Heathrow Airport.

Triumph Speed Twin

Many of Britain's early motorbike firms had origins in the bicycle trade, but Triumph was unusual in that it was a bicycle firm founded by two Germans. Siegfried Bettmann began by importing sewing machines, moved to exporting bicycles, and produced his first motorcycle, powered by a 2hp Minerva engine from Belgium, in 1902. By this time he had formed a partnership with an engineer named Mauritz Schulte, and they had changed the firm's name to Triumph.

*T*HREE YEARS later Triumph produced its own 363cc, 3hp side-valve engine, also moving away from the original bicycle-style frame to a lower diamond frame design. This and subsequent singles proved reliable and well-built, earning the nickname 'Trusty Triumph'. Jack Marshall rode a slightly modified machine to second place at the TT in 1907, and a year later went one better to win the single-cylinder class, with five more Triumphs in the top ten.

Early experiments with twin-cylinder prototypes were abandoned in 1914 in favour of the Model H, a 550cc four-stroke single with three-speed gearbox and belt final drive. It was much used by the British Army in the First World War, and was the mainstay of Triumph production for the next few years, along with the Junior, a simple 225cc two-stroke.

The Coventry firm's most innovative early model was the Model R, designed by Harry (later Sir Harry) Ricardo. Modifying the side-valve Model H with a four-valve cylinder head and central spark plug gave the 'Riccy' greatly improved performance, boosting top speed to 75mph (121km/h).

Below left: Early Triumphs earned the nickname 'trusty', but this 1912 machine appears in need of assistance.

Right: Edward Turner's Speed Twin, launched in 1937, triggered the British motorcycle industry's move to parallel twins.

SPECIFICATIONS	TRIUMPH SPEED TWIN (1937)
Engine	Air-cooled ohv four-valve parallel twin
Capacity	498cc (63 x 80mm)
Maximum power	27bhp @ 6000rpm
Transmission	Four-speed, chain final drive
Frame	Girder front forks; rigid rear
Suspension	Leaf-spring front and rear
Brakes	Drum front and rear
Weight	365lb (166kg)
Top speed	90mph (145km/h)

In 1924 Triumph shocked the motorcycle world when it launched the 500cc side-valve Model P. This was not because of an exceptional specification but because of its price. At under £45 the Model P sold for less than many rival 500cc models cost to build. Although performance was fairly modest, it quickly became very popular, with production levels reaching 1000 per week in 1925, and its success put some smaller firms out of business.

Triumph itself hit financial problems in the Depression of the 1930s. In 1936 the firm was sold to Ariel, whose owner Jack Sangster appointed Edward Turner as chief designer. The youthful Turner's first act was to revamp Triumph's Val Page-designed 500cc, 350cc and 250cc single-cylinder range, giving them silver-and-

chrome petrol tanks, upswept exhausts, new frames and catchy names: the Tiger 90, 80 and 70.

Meanwhile Turner was creating the machine that would revolutionize the industry and for which he would ever be remembered: the Speed Twin. The handsome 500cc parallel twin rapidly became a hit and was primarily responsible for the British industry's concerted move to twins. Its 27bhp ohv pushrod engine gave an impressive top speed of 90mph (145km/h) plus lively acceleration, and it was notably smoother than rival singles. The Speed Twin, which used the Tiger 90 chassis, was also light, compact and competitively priced.

Triumph moved fast to follow up the Speed Twin, and two years later introduced the Tiger 100, a sports model whose 33bhp engine really could provide the 100mph (161km/h) performance suggested by its name. Both models were successful in slightly revised form after the Second World War, and would form the basis of the Triumph range for the next 50 years.

In 1950, largely to satisfy US market demand for increased capacity, Triumph stretched the engine to 650cc to produce the 6T Thunderbird. The bike was another hit (boosted in 1954 when

ridden by Marlon Brando's character Johnny in the cult film *The Wild One*), and its capacity would remain a Triumph favourite. As a contemporary test put it, 'The riding characteristics leave nothing to be desired and if it's acceleration you crave, there are few stock, fully-equipped machines that could jerk your cork if you're on a Triumph Thunderbird.'

Above: The torquey 650cc Thunderbird was another Triumph success.

Triumph Bonneville

Triumph's best-loved twin, the 650cc Bonneville, was launched in 1959 and was a direct descendent of the Speed Twin of 22 years earlier. Numerous modifications over the years had seen the original 500cc parallel twin engine updated and enlarged, culminating in the 650cc Tiger 110 of 1954. This in turn could be tweaked with factory tuning parts, including a cylinder head with splayed inlet ports, for fitment of twin Amal racing carbs, and high-performance camshafts.

Below: Few Triumph enthusiasts can agree on which year and type of Bonneville is the best, but the 650cc T120R of 1961 would get plenty of votes.

Opposite left: Triumph produced the Silver Jubilee version of the 750cc T140 Bonneville in 1977. Opposite right: The T120R was light and rigid enough to corner pretty well.

*I*N 1959 TRIUMPH specified the hot cams and twin, filterless Amals as standard fitment to create the new T120 Bonneville whose output, of 46bhp at 6500rpm, made it 4bhp more powerful than the Tiger. Initially the Bonneville, which was conceived in such a hurry that it wasn't even included in Triumph's 1959 catalogue, looked almost identical to the Tiger with its headlamp nacelle (a one-year-only item), swept-back touring handlebars and large mudguards.

The name Bonneville was chosen by Triumph boss Edward Turner in honour of the record-breaking run by Johnny Allen, who in 1956 had taken a streamlined, Triumph twin-engined machine to 214mph (344km/h) at the Bonneville salt flats in Utah, USA. Although Triumph's claims to the world speed record were dismissed by the FIM (motorcycle sport's governing body) on a technicality, the firm gained much valuable publicity from the attempt, particularly in the all-important American market.

As well as having punchy acceleration and a 110mph (177km/h) top speed, the Bonnie was reasonably smooth, and it sold well. But its power was sometimes too much for the single-downtube frame, making the bike prone to high-speed wobbles. For 1960 Triumph introduced a new twin-cradle frame with steeper steering geometry and shorter wheelbase, plus improved front forks and new styling that incorporated a separate headlamp shell and smaller mudguards.

The Bonneville was regularly updated over the next decade and was built in several different forms, with the basic home-market T120 model joined by the T120C competition bike and a stylish if less practical export model with high bars and smaller petrol tank. In 1963, the factory introduced its new 'unit construction' 650 with its engine and gearbox combined, instead of employing the previous separate, or pre-unit, layout.

In 1951 Triumph had been bought by the BSA Group, but the marques remained separate until 1968, when a joint research establishment was set up at Umberslade Hall. Three years later this resulted in the introduction of the tall 'oil-in-frame' chassis, which was much criticized and promptly lowered. By now the British industry was facing increasing competition from Japan, but the Bonneville, in particular, could fight back. John Hartle proved its speed by winning the first Production TT in 1967; two years later Malcolm Uphill won again for Triumph, averaging 99.99mph (160.9km/h) and setting the first 'ton-up' lap in the process.

In 1973 capacity was increased to 744cc, producing the torquier but slightly more vibration-prone T140 Bonneville. The twin was also available as the Tiger, essentially identical except for its single carburettor. (There was also a police version, the Saint – the name standing, it was said, for 'stops anything in no time'.) But parent company Norton Villiers Triumph was in trouble. Amid rumours that the Meriden factory was about to close, workers staged an 18-month sit-in, after which production was restarted by a workers' co-operative.

Despite lack of development funds some improvements were made to the ageing twin, which was given an electric starter and an eight-valve cylinder head in the early 1980s. But by now the air-cooled pushrod unit was old-fashioned and uncompetitive. Triumph finally went into liquidation in 1983, after which it was bought by current owner John Bloor. He allowed Devon-based parts specialist Racing Spares to resurrect the Bonneville and build it under licence, but production ceased in 1988 after about 1200 bikes had been built.

SPECIFICATIONS	TRIUMPH T120 BONNEVILLE (1959)
Engine	Air-cooled ohv four-valve parallel twin
Capacity	649cc (71 x 82mm)
Maximum power	46bhp @ 6500rpm
Transmission	Four-speed, chain final drive
Frame	Steel single downtube
Suspension	Telescopic front; twin shocks rear
Brakes	Drum front and rear
Weight	403lb (183kg)
Top speed	110mph (177km/h)

Triumph Trident

Triumph began development of a three-cylinder roadster in 1965, and a roadgoing prototype was demonstrated to the police at the end of that year. But the project was delayed, largely due to opposition from the American importer – the United States was Triumph's biggest market in the 1960s.

Below: The T150 Trident had speed and handling, but lacked style and sophistication.
Opposite left: Despite good looks and improved performance, the T160 Trident couldn't save Triumph.
Opposite right: For pure style there was nothing to touch the 750 Hurricane.

*A*FTER FIRSTLY opposing the triple's creation altogether, the Americans demanded numerous styling changes and insisted that two separate models should be produced by Triumph and its sister firm BSA, whose Rocket Three eventually appeared at the same time.

When the Trident was finally launched, its slab-sided styling and unusual aquamarine paint scheme were unpopular. The 740cc triple engine had pushrod valve operation, and produced 58bhp at 7250rpm. Its chassis was heavily based on that of Triumph's twins, including the frame which was a strengthened version of their steel, single-downtube unit. Gaitered forks, borrowed directly from the twins, were given stiffer springs to help the suspension cope with the T150's extra weight.

The first Trident was very quick by the standards of its day. Its 125mph (201km/h) top speed and sub-14-second standing quarter mile time were a match for any bike on the roads in 1969, including Honda's new CB750, and the triple also handled well. Unfortunately the British bike couldn't match either the Japanese four's specification, which included a disc brake and electric starter, or its reliability, and it was not the success that Triumph had hoped for.

American influence resulted in the most stylish triple, in the wasp-waisted form of the X-75 Hurricane of 1973. The bike was commissioned by Triumph America and created by young freelance designer Craig Vetter, initially without the factory's knowledge. With its swoopy tank-seat unit and trio of shiny tailpipes on the right side, the Hurricane was a strikingly futuristic machine. Its

Slippery Sam

The Trident provided Triumph with some notable racing victories in the 1970s, not least in the Isle of Man, where the legendary production racer known as Slippery Sam won five consecutive TTs from 1971 to '75. The 1971 season was memorable for Triumph and BSA, whose race teams ran similar Rob North-framed triples. Dick Mann led a British one-two-three at Daytona in the USA, bringing his BSA home ahead of Triumph's Gene Romero. It was a magnificent last stand for the triples, soon to be outclassed by Yamaha's two-strokes.

Right: The most famous Trident was Slippery Sam, which dominated the TT Production race in the early 1970s.

lower-geared triple motor ensured that it was quick, too. Fewer than 1200 were produced, but the X–75 remains one of the most memorable of 1970s bikes.

Financial problems meant that a potentially more important development, the four-cylinder Quadrant prototype that engineer Doug Hele created in 1972, was not followed up. But Triumph created a handsome machine when relaunching the standard triple as the T160 Trident in 1975. Completely restyled and with more

than 200 mechanical modifications, the T160 belatedly dragged Triumph into the modern era. But it could hardly have been introduced at a more difficult time for parent group Norton Villiers Triumph, which had made a loss of several million pounds in the previous year.

In those circumstances, the T160, which was built not at Meriden but at the BSA factory in Small Heath, Birmingham, was a surprisingly good bike. Its engine incorporated a number of updated features including an electric starter and left-foot gearchange. Unlike the vertical T150 motor, but in common with BSA's similar Rocket 3, the T160's engine was angled forward in a new steel frame, the layout of which owed much to Triumph's works production racers.

The T160 backed up its handsome new styling by proving a fast, reasonably smooth, and fine-handling superbike. Despite a high price and some unreliability, the new triple was popular. But NVT's deepening financial problems brought the end for the Small Heath factory and the Trident. The final triples, white-finished Cardinal police models bound for Saudi Arabia, were assembled in December 1975.

SPECIFICATIONS	TRIUMPH T150 TRIDENT (1969)
Engine	Air-cooled ohv six-valve triple
Capacity	740cc (67 x 70mm)
Maximum power	58bhp @ 7250rpm
Transmission	Four-speed, chain final drive
Frame	Steel single downtube
Suspension	Telescopic front; twin shocks rear
Brakes	Drum front and rear
Weight	468lb (212kg)
Top speed	125mph (201km/h)

Triumph Trophy 1200

The most significant moment in the recent history of the British motorcycle industry came when John Bloor, a Midlands-based multi-millionaire who had made his fortune by building houses, decided to produce motorbikes too.

Below left: Triumph's four-cylinder Trophy 1200 sports-tourer was remarkably competitive with its Japanese opposition.
Below right: The base-model Trident triple was great fun, especially in its 900cc capacity.

*T*RIUMPH, THE last of the great old firms, had apparently lost its struggle for survival. The once mighty British bike industry was dead – or so most people assumed. But Bloor bought Triumph from the liquidator in 1983, and spent the next eight years secretly developing a range of modern machines in a purpose-built factory at Hinckley in Leicestershire, just a few miles from the old Meriden site.

In 1991, Bloor's reborn Triumph stunned the motorcycle world by launching a range of six superbikes with capacities ranging from 750cc to 1200cc. Their basic engine layout owed much to Japanese design but incorporated a unique modular concept. Using three or four cylinders plus a choice of short- or long-stroke crankshafts, Triumph produced four different engines and a total of six models, all using the same steel spine frame. The modular concept bore an obvious similarity to a plan that BSA-Triumph engineer Bert Hopwood had devised in the 1970s, but which, in the event, had not been put into production.

Triumph's basic roadster model was the Trident, a naked triple available in 749cc or 885cc capacity. Like all the new bikes, it combined its steel spine frame with suspension and brake components from Japan. It looked good, it handled well and it was great fun to ride, especially the larger-engined version, which produced 98bhp, had lots of midrange torque, and stormed to a top speed of 130mph (209km/h).

The Daytona sports machines, handicapped by the modular concept, struggled to compete with more specialized Japanese race-replicas, but the flagship Trophy 1200 was a very impressive sports-tourer. Its four-cylinder engine was effectively the triple unit with an extra pot. The twin-cam, 16-valve motor produced a maximum of 125bhp at 9000rpm. Although it owed much to Japanese influence (rumours of a link with Kawasaki took some time to die), the engine was designed and built in Hinckley.

It was a compliment to Triumph's thorough development work that the Trophy was immediately competitive with top-class sports-

tourers such as Kawasaki's ZZ-R1100 and Honda's CBR1000F. The British bike was smooth and fast, surging to over 150mph (241km/h), and its flexible power delivery and comfortable, fully-faired riding position made for relaxed long-distance travel. Triumph's somewhat dated spine-framed chassis was very efficient, too, giving the Trophy excellent stability and light steering.

Triumph rapidly established itself in the home market. Exports began rather slowly, due partly to sales resistance in Germany. But

crucially the new Triumphs proved to be well-built and reliable, and soon the Hinckley factory was expanding as new export markets were developed, and annual production rose towards 10,000 bikes.

The three-cylinder models were generally better received than the less distinctive fours, and Triumph became skilful at exploiting its tradition with carefully targeted models. The Speed Triple, launched in 1994, was a stylish naked roadster that combined the Trident's 885cc triple engine with clip-on handlebars, top-class suspension and fat radial tyres. Its aggressive look and riding position, along with 130mph (209km/h) top speed and excellent handling, made the Speed Triple the natural successor to the café racers of the 1960s.

A year later Triumph played the nostalgia card more emphatically with the Thunderbird, a retro-styled cruiser complete with traditional 'mouth-organ' tank badge. Triumph retained the modular frame but added wire-spoked wheels and a lower seat, and developed the 885cc triple engine with exaggerated cooling fins and a reduced 69bhp power output. The public loved the look, and the Thunderbird became Triumph's best-selling model worldwide.

Above: Triumph's designers exploited the firm's heritage with the stylish Thunderbird triple cruiser in 1995.

Above: Mean naked looks and a potent 885cc engine earned the Speed Triple plenty of admirers.

SPECIFICATIONS	TRIUMPH TROPHY 1200 (1991)
Engine	Liquid-cooled dohc 16-valve four
Capacity	1180cc (76 x 65mm)
Maximum power	125bhp @ 9000rpm
Transmission	Six-speed, chain final drive
Frame	Steel spine
Suspension	Telescopic front; single shock rear
Brakes	Twin disc front; disc rear
Weight	529lb (240kg)
Top speed	153mph (246km/h)

Triumph T595 Daytona

The second phase of Triumph's remarkable recovery came in 1997, with the release of the T595 Daytona. Here for the first time was a British bike designed to compete head-on with the Japanese and Italians in the glamorous large-capacity super-sports class. For Triumph, that meant abandoning the modular concept on which its growth had been based, in favour of an all-new machine.

Below: With its striking looks, thrilling performance and fine handling, the T595 Daytona proved that Triumph could build a top-class sports bike.
Opposite: The Thunderbird Sport; performance with retro style.
Opposite below: Many experienced testers rated the Sprint ST the world's best sports-tourer.

*P*OWER CAME from a 955cc three-cylinder engine based on the original 885cc, 12-valve triple. Lotus Engineering helped tune the motor, mainly with improved breathing. A sophisticated French-made fuel-injection system replaced the old model's carburettors, feeding the engine via larger, lighter valves operated by new camshafts.

Triumph's traditional steel spine frame was abandoned in favour of an eye-catching design featuring twin oval-section aluminium tubes. A single-sided aluminium swing-arm added a

further stylish touch. With a sleek twin-headlamp fairing in yellow or black, and a racy riding position dictated by clip-on handlebars and rearset footrests, the T595 was an unashamedly aggressive machine in looks and performance.

Following its launch at the Cologne Show in 1996, the T595 Daytona was in huge demand, particularly in Britain. (Its name, taken from the factory codename in Triumph tradition, confused some people who thought it referred to 595cc capacity, and was later changed to Daytona 955i.) The tuned triple motor was

torquey and powerful, sending the Triumph storming smoothly towards a top speed of over 160mph (257km/h).

And the new British challenger handled superbly, too. Its rigid frame, well damped suspension and light weight combined to give unshakeable stability and very neutral steering. Its disc brakes were powerful, its fat radial tyres sticky. The Triumph did not quite match the agility and sheer speed of more narrowly focused superbikes such as Honda's FireBlade, but as a high-performance roadgoing sportster it was right up there with the very best.

Two years later Triumph attacked the sports-tourer market with the Sprint ST, and produced a bike that was arguably even more impressive. The new triple had much in common with the Daytona. Its engine was detuned with revised fuel-injection, camshafts and exhaust system to give increased midrange performance while reducing peak output to 110bhp.

The Sprint became the first Triumph to use a twin-beam aluminium frame, which was cheaper to produce and more rigid than the Daytona's tubular aluminium structure. (Triumph had also had some problems with cracking of the tubular frame, but had earned customer respect with a conscientious and expensive policy

of replacement.) The single-sided swing-arm and brakes were borrowed from the sports bike.

Styling was less aggressive than the Daytona's due partly to a taller screen. Its riding position was designed for comfort as well as speed, with slightly raised handlebars, a broad seat and plenty of legroom, but the Sprint still provided plenty of excitement. Its 12-valve motor combined midrange punch with enough smooth, high-revving power for a top speed of over 150mph (241km/h).

When ridden hard the Sprint couldn't match the handling precision of more firmly suspended super-sports bikes. But the Triumph was light for a sports-tourer, and its suspension, brakes and tyres were excellent. Equally importantly, the triple was comfortable, well-finished, comprehensively equipped (with optional matching luggage) and competitively priced.

The Sprint ST was not merely a fine sports-tourer, it was arguably better than Honda's ultra-sophisticated VFR800FI, the class yardstick – a judgement delivered by magazine comparison tests not just in Britain, but all over the world. Its arrival capped a sensational decade for Triumph, and for a British motorcycle industry that had so recently seemed dead and buried.

SPECIFICATIONS	TRIUMPH T595 DAYTONA (1997)
Engine	Liquid-cooled dohc 12-valve triple
Capacity	955cc (79 x 65mm)
Maximum power	128bhp @ 10,200rpm
Transmission	Six-speed, chain final drive
Frame	Tubular aluminium perimeter
Suspension	Telescopic front; single shock rear
Brakes	Twin disc front; single disc rear
Weight	436lb (198kg)
Top speed	165mph (266km/h)

Velocette KSS

Sporty singles were Veloce Ltd's most notable product, from the mid-1920s to the closure of the family firm in 1971. Most were finished in black with gold pinstriping, many were cleverly engineered and very fast, and a good number were raced with great success. World road-race championships, TT victories and endurance records all added to the Birmingham marque's rich history.

Below: Velocette's best loved roadster of the 1930s was the KSS, the race-developed overhead-cam 350cc single that offered an attractive blend of speed and handling.

*V*ELOCETTE CAME to personify a distinctly English style of motorcycling but, like Triumph, the firm had German origins. Johannes Gütgemann moved to Britain in the 1880s, and changed his name to John Taylor. He began in business by making pills and, after diversifying into bicycle manufacture, he set up a motorcycle firm in 1904. That failed, but Taylor (who later changed the family name to Goodman) tried again in 1910, operating as Veloce with his sons Percy and Eugene.

Percy designed the firm's first model, a 276cc four-stroke single, but it was the 206cc two-stroke single launched in 1913 that brought the firm its early success. This lightweight economy machine was the first bike marketed as a Velocette. It was sold in three versions: direct belt drive, two-speed chain drive, and a ladies' version of the two-speed, with a lower frame. After the First World War the two-stroke remained popular, and it was refined over the years with a larger 220cc and 249cc engine, three-speed gearbox, clutch, front brake and kickstart.

Percy Goodman's masterpiece was the 350cc overhead-cam ('Cammy') single released in 1925. Introduced as a Veloce but rapidly rebadged Velocette, this used bevel drive to its camshaft, was capable of an impressive 70mph (113km/h) in standard form, and soon brought racing success. Alec Bennett won the 1926 Junior TT, finishing no less than ten minutes ahead of the next-placed rider. This was followed by a second place in the Junior the following

SPECIFICATIONS	VELOCETTE KSS Mk II (1936)
Engine	Air-cooled ohc two-valve single
Capacity	348cc (74 x 81mm)
Maximum power	25bhp approx
Transmission	Four-speed, chain final drive
Frame	Steel single downtube
Suspension	Girder front; rigid rear
Brakes	Drum front and rear
Weight	330lb (150kg) approx
Top speed	80mph (129km/h)

year, and two more wins (Bennett again, then Freddie Hicks) in 1928 and '29.

Bennett's first TT-winning machine was no more than a production roadster, known as the K model, tuned and fitted with a stronger clutch. In this form it was good for almost 90mph (145km/h), and averaged 66.7mph (107.3km/h) despite a last-lap crash. Velocette brought much of that performance to the street with the sporty KSS single, which combined respectable straight-line speed with outstanding handling.

Along the way it gained various modifications, notably the positive-stop, foot-operated gearchange devised by development engineer Harold Willis. This was introduced in 1929 on the firm's TT bikes, and on the KSS three years later, initially as an optional extra. In 1929 Velocette also took the unprecedented step of marketing an 'over-the-counter' racing machine. The KTT model introduced itself in a remarkable way by taking the first eight places at the 1930 Manx Grand Prix, and remained the ultimate clubman's machine for years to come.

Velocette scored another hit in 1930 with the launch of the GTP, a 249cc two-stroke with coil ignition, but what the firm really needed was a four-stoke that cost less to produce than the ohc models. Eugene Goodman's 250cc MOV, introduced in 1933, filled the gap in the range and was a big success. The high-cam pushrod motor was soon enlarged to 350cc, producing the MAC model, then to 495cc to give the MSS, whose chassis was strengthened for sidecar use.

In 1936 Velocette uprated the ohc range with the KSS Mk II. This combined a MAC-based chassis with an all-new engine, featuring an aluminium cylinder head and, for the first time, fully enclosed valvegear. (The old design was notoriously leaky.) Two versions were produced, the sporty KSS and the touring KTS, which had bigger mudguards and fatter tyres. They gave the 'cammy Velo' a new lease of life, and it remained in the range until 1948.

Above: The GTP, powered by a 250cc two-stroke engine with coil ignition, was a successful departure for Velocette in the 1930s.

Left: The pushrod-operated MAC was less glamorous and slower than its fellow 350cc single the KSS, but was also a lot less expensive to produce than the overhead-cam machine. The MAC remained in production well into the 1950s, when this bike was built.

Velocette Thruxton

Brothers Percy and Eugene Goodman had been running Velocette since the death of their father John in 1928. The company's post-war production centred on the sporty singles on which its reputation was based, but the firm also looked for alternatives.

Below: With its clip-on bars, rearset footrests, humped seat, gaping Amal racing carb and big front drum brake, the Venom Thruxton has the aggressive looks to match its hotted-up 500cc engine.

*W*HILE PERCY had concentrated on racing and the overhead-cam K series singles, Eugene had successfully introduced the simpler and more profitable pushrod M series bikes. But when he led Velocette towards lightweights, aimed at 'everyman' rather than enthusiasts, the results were very different.

The first evidence of this came in 1949 with the dramatic introduction of the LE, a novel machine that combined a pressed-steel frame and leg-shields with a 149cc, water-cooled flat-twin engine. The side-valve motor featured a hand-change gearbox and shaft final drive, and produced just 8bhp. That gave the LE (short for Little Engine), which at 260lb (118kg) was on the heavy side, a top speed of just 50mph (80km/h) and sluggish performance on hills.

In its favour the LE was well-built, smooth, comfortable, practical, quiet and handled well. But it was also strangely styled, relatively complicated and 50 per cent more expensive than BSA's Bantam. Sales were disastrously low, even after a 1951 capacity increase to 192cc had triggered the first of numerous purchases by police forces. The huge amount of money invested in the LE – its production equipment alone reportedly cost three good years' worth of profits – was wasted, and Velocette consequently revised plans to abandon production of the MAC 350cc single.

One of the casualties of the expense of tooling-up for the LE in the late Forties was Velocette's racing effort, which was scaled down despite some notable successes in previous years. The FIM's

Left: By 1961, when this bike was built, the LE's flat-twin engine had grown to 192cc, but sales of the strangely styled machine remained disastrously low.

Below: The failure of the Viceroy, powered by a 250cc flat-twin two-stroke, pushed Velocette ever closer to extinction.

post-war ban on supercharging had put paid to the 'Roarer', a 500cc supercharged parallel twin that had been debuted by Stanley Woods at the 1939 TT. But Woods had won the Junior TT in 1938 and '39. And despite the budget cuts, Velocette continued to dominate when racing resumed after the war.

The firm's KTT Mk VIII, the ultimate version of its famous over-the-counter production racer, dated from 1938. The 34bhp single was almost identical to Woods' TT-winning factory machine of that year, and was still competitive a decade later. Bob Foster and Freddie Frith rode it to a hat-trick of post-war Junior TT wins. And when the world championships began, Frith and Foster took the first two titles (in 1949 and '50 respectively) on factory dohc or 'double-knocker' versions of the Mk VIII.

By this time the ohc KSS roadster had been dropped, but in 1956 Velocette introduced a new pair of sporty pushrod singles, the 500cc Venom and 350cc Viper. Both were available in higher-performance Clubman specification, and the larger-engined version

of this led, in the mid-1960s, to the bike that remains for many the ultimate roadgoing Velocette: the Thruxton.

Essentially a tuned Venom Clubman, the Thruxton was built to commemorate a 1964 victory in the prestigious 500-mile race at the Hampshire track of that name. Its engine mods included big valves, high-compression pistons and hot cams, plus an Amal racing carb that helped lift peak output to 40bhp. Clip-ons and rearsets, a big tank, humped seat, firmer suspension and big twin-leading-shoe drum brake completed a handsome roadburner that handled superbly and was good for over 100mph (161km/h) in road trim.

If the Thruxton was classical Velocette, several of the firm's other models of the 1950s and '60s were anything but. The LE disaster had been compounded by the Valiant, an unreliable overhead-valve variant launched in 1956, and the Vogue, a fully enclosed model with similar 200cc flat-twin engine. The Viceroy, a scooter with a 250cc flat-twin two-stroke engine, was equally unsuccessful, and Velocette went into liquidation in 1971.

SPECIFICATIONS	VELOCETTE VENOM THRUXTON (1965)
Engine	Air-cooled ohv two-valve single
Capacity	499cc (86 x 86mm)
Maximum power	40bhp @ 6200rpm
Transmission	Four-speed, chain final drive
Frame	Steel single downtube
Suspension	Telescopic front; twin shocks rear
Brakes	Drum front and rear
Weight	390lb (177kg)
Top speed	105mph (169km/h)

Vincent

The fastest and most glamorous motorbikes of the 1950s were the thundering V-twins built by Vincent, the small firm from Stevenage in Hertfordshire. Created with little regard to cost, they were handsome, cleverly engineered and beautifully finished machines whose performance remained unmatched long after Vincent production had ended. They remain hugely desirable today.

Below: Handsome looks and thunderous performance make the Black Shadow an all-time great.

Opposite left: The Shadow's black-finished V-twin engine was tuned to give 55bhp.

Opposite right: The Black Prince was fast and practical, but lacked the naked V-twins' grace.

*P*HILIP CONRAD Vincent grew up on his parents' cattle range in Argentina. He was an engineering student at Cambridge University when, in 1927, he persuaded his father to fund the construction of a prototype bike of his own design, powered by a 350cc MAG engine. Shortly afterwards he left Cambridge and set up a motorcycle business.

In 1928, Vincent bought the name of HRD Motors. The initials were those of Howard Davies, who had won the TT three years earlier, but whose bike-building firm had failed. Vincent thought the name would give his new company credibility, although virtually the only HRD feature he retained was its paint scheme of black with gold trim.

Vincent-HRD began building bikes using engines from firms including Villiers, JAP and Rudge. Vincent and his Australian chief engineer Phil Irving used 'special' JAP engines for the company's first entry in the TT in 1934, but all three Vincent riders retired with mechanical problems. After returning from the Isle of Man, the pair designed an innovative 500cc high-camshaft single-cylinder engine in just three months. The 1935-model Vincent Comet was good for 90mph (145km/h), and Vincent never built a bike with a bought-in engine again.

Legend has it that Irving's inspiration for the first Vincent V-twin came when two drawings of the single engine were blown into a Vee shape by a breeze. True or not, in 1936 he combined two

Comet cylinders at 47 degrees to produce a 998cc, 45bhp V-twin – the Rapide. Nicknamed the 'Snarling Beast', and less kindly the 'plumber's nightmare' because of its external oil lines, the 110mph (177km/h) Rapide was supremely fast, but its torque led to transmission problems.

Vincent replaced it after the Second World War with the improved Series B Rapide. Its new unit-construction V-twin motor had cylinders placed at 50 degrees, and it formed a stressed member of the chassis, meaning no downtubes were needed. Combining effortless high-speed cruising ability with good handling from its more compact chassis, and powerful braking from twin drums on each wheel, the Series B Rapide was the finest bike of its day.

Vincent's greatest roadster of all was the Black Shadow, which was launched in 1948 powered by a tuned, 55bhp black-finished engine. Its large Smiths speedometer was calibrated to 150mph (241km/h), and the mighty Shadow was capable of over 120mph (193km/h). A year later Vincent introduced the Series C range, in touring Rapide, sports Black Shadow and racing Black Lightning forms. Vincent Girdraulic forks replaced the previous Brampton girders; the thundering V-twins' reputation for unmatched performance remained.

In the early 1950s the big V-twins were proving unprofitable, even at the high prices charged, and the receiver was called in. Production continued, and the firm branched out by assembling Firefly engines and NSU lightweight bikes under licence. New Series D Vincents, the Black Knight and tuned Black Prince, featured all-enveloping fibreglass bodywork and received a mixed reception when launched in 1955. By the end of the year, Vincent production had ended.

Vincent's Record-Breakers

Vincents broke many speed records over the years, most famously in 1949 at Bonneville, Utah, when Rollie Free, riding a tuned Black Lightning V-twin, stripped to swimming trunks and shoes to set a world record for unsupercharged bikes at 150.313mph (241.89km/h).

Other legendary Vincents included Gunga Din, Nero and the supercharged Super Nero, on which George Brown set speed records and won numerous sprints and hillclimbs. Bob Burns and Russell Wright set a string of sidecar and solo world records in New Zealand in the mid-1950s, with Wright eventually being clocked at over 190mph (306km/h).

SPECIFICATIONS	VINCENT BLACK SHADOW SERIES C (1949)
Engine	Air-cooled ohv four-valve 50-degree V-twin
Capacity	998cc (84 x 90mm)
Maximum power	55bhp @ 5700rpm
Transmission	Four-speed, chain final drive
Frame	Steel spine
Suspension	Girder front; twin shocks rear
Brakes	Twin drums front and rear
Weight	458lb (208kg)
Top speed	125mph (201km/h)

Wilkinson

Few early machines approached the sophistication of the Wilkinson, which appeared in 1909 featuring an in-line four-cylinder engine, shaft final drive, front and rear suspension and a luxurious bucket seat. Given its exotic specification and upmarket touring image, the bike's background was particularly strange, for it had been conceived as a military scouting machine by its makers, the well-known manufacturer of swords (and more recently razor blades).

Below left: Most Wilkinson fours had conventional handlebars, but at least one example of the in-line four was fitted with a car-style steering wheel.

Below right: The 848cc water-cooled version of the four was introduced in 1912.

*D*ESIGNER P.G. Tacchi's creation had been powered by a transverse-mounted V-twin engine and fitted with a Maxim machine-gun on its handlebars when demonstrated to the Army authorities – apparently without success – in 1908. When launched as a luxury civilian machine a year later, it had gained the 676cc four-cylinder motor, and was named the TAC, standing for Touring Auto Cycle. As if the bike were not eccentric enough when fitted with conventional handlebars, it was also produced with a steering wheel!

For 1912 the Wilkinson was uprated with an 848cc water-cooled engine, with side-valves in place of the previous automatic inlet valve layout. This model was known as the TMC, or Touring Motor Cycle. Saxon girder forks replaced the earlier Wilkinson or Druid units, and the 320lb (145kg) TMC's rear wheel was suspended using a leaf-spring arrangement. There was no front brake, but a foot-pedal operated twin drums on the rear wheel.

In 1913 Wilkinson Sword became involved in producing a light car called the Deemster, powered by a 996cc four-cylinder engine,

and the bike was also fitted with the new motor for use with a sidecar. The firm's own chair was a typically upmarket affair, and employed parallel leaf-spring suspension similar to that of the motorcycle. When the First World War broke out in the following year, Wilkinson Sword dropped vehicle production to concentrate on swords and bayonets. Engine production for the Deemster car resumed after the war, but the bike project was not restarted.

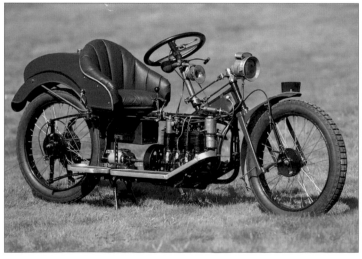

SPECIFICATIONS	WILKINSON TMC (1912)
Engine	Liquid-cooled side-valve eight-valve in-line four
Capacity	848cc (60 x 75mm)
Maximum power	Not known
Transmission	Three-speed, shaft final drive
Frame	Steel twin downtube
Suspension	Girder front; leaf-spring rear
Brakes	No front; twin drum rear
Weight	320lb (145kg)
Top speed	Not known

Williamson

Billy Williamson founded Rex with his brother Harold at the turn of the century, but in 1911 both left the firm after a boardroom split. While Harold found work with the Singer motorcycle company, Billy set up on his own, backed by William Douglas, owner of the well-established Bristol-based firm. Billy's first prototype machine, developed in conjunction with William Douglas Junior, appeared in 1912 under the name Williamson-Douglas.

Above: The 964cc flat-twin engine was liquid-cooled.
Below: The Douglas flat-twin engine had been intended for use in a machine called the Cyclecar, but worked well enough as a motorcycle powerplant. Wilkinson also built a handful of bikes with JAP V-twin engines.

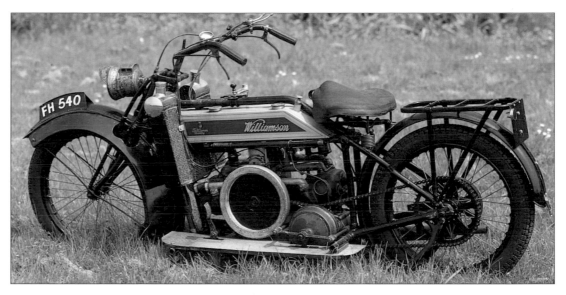

Above: 1914 Williamson Douglas car engine 1000cc.

THE ARRANGEMENT suited both parties, for although Douglas bike production was based around 350cc flat-twins, the firm was also set to begin building the Cyclecar, powered by a liquid-cooled, 964cc flat-twin. This motor was also well suited to a motorcycle intended for use with a sidecar, helping Douglas spread the costs of development. Douglas sent engines to Williamson's base in Coventry, where the new bike was assembled. Its blue tank panels carried Coventry's elephant-and-lynx coat of arms.

The Williamson was a fairly well-specified machine with a two-speed Douglas gearbox, foot-operated clutch and hand-change on the top of the petrol tank. The twin was suspended at the front by Douglas-Druid girder forks, whose pair of side-mounted springs worked in tension. Braking was hardly the bike's strong point, as its 300lb (136kg) weight was halted by no more than a bicycle-style stirrup front brake, and a heel-operated contracting band at the rear.

Williamson uprated the twin in various ways during the next couple of years, and also produced an air-cooled version that sold

for £75 against the original's £82. But the First World War halted production in 1914, and when peace returned the Douglas motor was no longer available. Williamson redesigned the bike to take a 980cc JAP side-valve motor, but had built only a small number before suffering a fatal heart attack in 1920. Production of the Williamson did not continue.

SPECIFICATIONS	WILLIAMSON (1913)
Engine	Liquid-cooled side-valve four-valve flat-twin
Capacity	964cc (85 x 85mm)
Maximum power	Not known
Transmission	Two-speed, chain final drive
Frame	Steel duplex cradle
Suspension	Girder front; rigid rear
Brakes	Stirrup front; contracting band rear
Weight	300lb (136kg)
Top speed	55mph (88km/h) approx

Zenith

Bikes bearing the Zenith name were built for more than 40 years, but the marque will always be best remembered for one of its earliest inventions: the Zenith Gradua gear system. This was created in 1908 by Freddie Barnes, Zenith's ace designer, and gave the firm's machines a big advantage over rivals with fixed gearing (which meant all of them), especially in hillclimb competitions.

Below: The Gradua system helped this 550cc JAP-engined V-twin, which was built in 1914, to pull a sidecar, though with only 6hp to call on, progress was sedate.

*U*NTIL THE Gradua's arrival, the belt-drive bikes of the day had to have their gearing altered by adjusting the position of the crankshaft pulley that took drive to the rear wheel. The trouble was that if the belt was correctly tensioned in high gear, it was hopelessly slack in low. The Gradua got round this by using a long handle, known as the 'coffee grinder', which was connected to both the pulley and the rear-wheel spindle. Turning the coffee-grinder moved both pulley and spindle, altering gearing while keeping the belt in tension. Eureka!

The system was not perfect, as the belt was prone to slip at times, especially in wet weather, and the rear brake's efficiency varied with wheel position. But generally it was a big advantage. The Gradua gave such an edge in hillclimbs that Barnes won 53 events in 1911, and 58 the following year, after which the ACU banned the device from single-speed events.

This delighted Zenith's management, who responded by using the word 'Barred' in a publicity campaign, and creating a new logo that depicted a motorbike imprisoned behind the bars of a jail. The logo continued to be used long after the Gradua had been superseded by the Rudge Multi and other gear systems.

The Zenith firm had begun in motorcycle production back in 1905, with an unusual two-wheeled device called the Tooley's

Bicar. This combined a 3hp Fafnir engine with a frame consisting of twin tubes linked by springs. One set of tubes supported the wheels; the other held the rider and engine platform. Steering was by a car-style hub-centre device. Little is known of its performance, but the Bicar was short-lived.

Zenith had much more success with its more conventional machines, especially when fitted with the Gradua. Early bikes were powered by a 482cc side-valve single from Fafnir, and from 1914 the firm used mainly JAP V-twin engines. In 1920 there was also a Bradshaw-engined flat-twin, and two years later Zenith introduced its first chain-drive bikes.

By 1928 Zenith's range comprised nine models, ranging from a 172cc Villiers-engined utility bike to a choice of three JAP-engined 680cc V-twins, the top model being the Super-Eight Sports. The capacity of 680cc had long been a Zenith favourite in both side-valve and ohv forms. The former was typically a touring model, and in 1928 the 'Six-Eighty' side-valve came fitted with a large spring-top saddle and the latest Druid girder forks.

Zenith also built high-performance bikes that were successful at Brooklands racetrack (at one stage the firm was based at nearby Weybridge in Surrey). Riding identical 998cc Zenith-JAP twins, Joe Wright and Oliver Baldwin were joint holders of the Brooklands track record at 113.45mph (182.58km/h) until Wright raised it further to 118.86mph (191.28km/h). But by 1930 the firm was struggling in the Depression, and the factory closed in that year.

SPECIFICATIONS	ZENITH GRADUA V-TWIN (1914)
Engine	Air-cooled side-valve four-valve V-twin
Capacity	550cc
Maximum power	6hp approx
Transmission	Gradua system; belt final drive
Frame	Steel single downtube
Suspension	Girder front; rigid rear
Brakes	Stirrup front; contracting band rear
Weight	Not known
Top speed	50mph (80km/h) approx

Writers of Kennington in South London, one of Zenith's biggest dealers, bought the name and recommended production before the Second World War intervened in 1939. When JAP failed to restart engine production after the war, Zenith was left with no viable alternatives. Writers built some bikes with its small remaining stock of 750cc V-twin engines, but once they were used up, the Zenith name disappeared.

Left: JAP V-twins were a Zenith favourite in the early years.

Below: This 678cc JAP-engined Gradua's "coffee-grinder" lever can be clearly seen.

Index